CAREERS FOR

TALKATIVE TYPES

& Others with the Gift of Gab

Careers for You Series

CAREERS FOR

TALKATIVE TYPES

& Others with the Gift of Gab

Marjorie Eberts
Margaret Gisler

SECOND EDITION

New York   Chicago   San Francisco   Lisbon   London   Madrid   Mexico City
Milan   New Delhi   San Juan   Seoul   Singapore   Sydney   Toronto

The *McGraw·Hill* Companies

Library of Congress Cataloging-in-Publication Data

Eberts, Marjorie.
    Careers for talkative types & others with the gift of gab / by Marjorie Eberts,
Margaret Gisler.— 2nd ed.
        p.   cm. — (McGraw-Hill careers for you series)
        ISBN 0-07-146779-3 (alk. paper)
        1. Vocational guidance—United States.   2. Professions—Vocational
guidance—United States.   3. Public relations—Vocational guidance—United
States.   4. Mass Media—Vocational guidance—United States.   5. Sales
personnel—Vocational guidance—United States.   I. Title: Careers for talkative
types and others with the gift of gab.   II. Gisler, Margaret.   III. Title.

HF5382.5 U5E24 2006
331.702—dc22   2006005698

1 2 3 4 5 6 7 8 9 0   DOC/DOC   0 9 8 7 6

ISBN-13: 978-0-07-146779-7
ISBN-10:   0-07-146779-3

McGraw-Hill books are available at special quantity discounts to use as premiums and
sales promotions, or for use in corporate training programs. For more information,
please write to the Director of Special Sales, Professional Publishing, McGraw-Hill,
Two Penn Plaza, New York, NY 10121-2298. Or contact your local bookstore.

This book is printed on acid-free paper.

*To my best friend, Sonia Fernandez Kevil,
whom I have talked to since we were
freshman roommates in college. What I
appreciate most about our conversations
is that throughout all the years, you have
continued to truly listen to me and reply
through thoughtful advice. I don't always
take the advice, but you always listen, and
I want to thank you for that. —MG*

Contents

CHAPTER ONE

Talk It Up!

Careers for Talkative Types

D o you truly enjoy chatting? Can you shoot the breeze about anything with anyone? Have people told you that you are articulate and have great communication skills? As a child did you eagerly wave your hand in class to answer any questions that teachers asked? Do you talk at length with salespeople? Would you consider an evening of conversation with friends to be a real treat? When people describe you to others, do they use words such as *chatterbox, motor mouth, gabby, jabberer,* or *loquacious*? If so, you are a talkative type, and, like all those with the gift of gab, you will be happiest working in a career where you can spend most of your time talking. You don't belong in a job in the "no talking" section of the library.

Your ability to talk is an asset that you can use in an amazing variety of careers. Having a way with words helped politicians such as Abraham Lincoln, John Kennedy, and Bill Clinton get elected to office. It's the funny patter of Rosie O'Donnell and Jerry Seinfeld that has propelled them to the top in the entertainment world. It is courtroom eloquence that has helped many present-day attorneys win high-profile cases. It is the persuasive words of salespeople that convince millions of people to buy cars, computers, shoes, houses, and insurance policies every day. It is the sage advice of psychologists and counselors that helps troubled people turn their lives around. Of course, in every one of these careers, it is not enough just to be able to jabber continually. What is essential is knowing what you are talking about. Teachers have to know the subject matter, whether they are teaching in kindergarten or in college. Ministers must be experts on the scriptures. Insurance salespeople have to understand the complex details of policies, just as stockbrokers must know all about bull and bear markets.

A Quick Look at Jobs for Talkative Types

Almost every job, from assembly-line worker to accountant to sculptor, is likely to require some talking. But talkative types want something more—the opportunity to spend the workday engaged in meaningful speech. Glance through the following want ads and you will see just a few of the many careers awaiting chatty people. Notice that every job is seeking someone who possesses solid communication skills.

RESTAURANT: Upscale café is seeking qualified lead hosts and hostesses with great experience and communication skills.

RECEPTIONIST: Real estate firm wants full-time receptionist. You will answer incoming calls, greet clients, and perform a variety of clerical duties. If you are a self-starter with excellent communication skills, please fax resume.

RECRUITER: Duties to include coordinating recruitment strategies, prescreening candidates, interviewing candidates for both technical and nontechnical positions, reference checking, and providing training. You will possess a human resources degree, excellent communication skills, computer skills, and considerable interviewing and recruiting experience.

SALES: Specialty clothing store needs salesperson with proven sales expertise, excellent communication skills, and a love of fashion.

MARKET RESEARCH SPECIALIST: Pharmaceutical company requires strong analytical communication, presentation, and writing skills and

a demonstrated ability to influence. Previous pharmaceutical experience and strong computer skills a plus.

SOCIAL WORKER: Mental health center is seeking a specialist in crisis intervention. Must have good crisis-management skills and
strong communication skills.

This book is designed to help talkative people discover jobs that
will pay them for talking. Here is a brief overview of some of the
jobs that you will read about in this book.

Glamour Talkers in the Limelight

If you see yourself becoming a comedian, a radio talk-show host,
or a performer on television, you will need to be extremely facile
with words. In fact, your success in these jobs in the limelight is
largely based on your way with words. You must use words to cap-
ture and hold the attention of the people in your audience,
whether you are attempting to inform, educate, or amuse them.
Jobs in this profession are not limited to the big names we all
know, such as Jay Leno, Oprah Winfrey, or Rush Limbaugh; there
are hundreds of jobs with local and regional radio and television
stations for those of you who have an especially appealing way
with words.

Sales Talkers

Whenever a product or service is sold, there is a salesperson
nearby who has used his or her gift of gab to influence the sale. If
you have the personality and desire to sell, you will usually be able
to get a job as a salesperson even if you only have a high school
diploma. Of course, to sell some scientific, technological, or
industrial products, you will need the special knowledge that
comes from a college degree in science or engineering. As a salesperson, your workplace can range from a store in a mall to a large
territory that requires considerable traveling. Before you begin

any sales job, you will receive some training. It may be as simple as on-the-job instruction from a supervisor or as formal as a program lasting up to two years. No matter where you work, the key to success in this career is the number of sales you make.

Talkers in Businesses and Other Organizations

Talkers in businesses and other organizations are the people who meet the public. The first person on the firing line is the receptionist, who sets the tone for how a business or organization is perceived. Then there are the marketing people, who play a crucial role in selling products or services, while the public relations employees garner publicity. Finally, there are all the human resources people, who spend their days talking to people as they try to find just the right new employees. In these jobs, what you say and how you say it will have a definite effect on the success of the business or organization where you work.

Telephone Talkers

So many people love to spend their free time gabbing on the phone. This love affair with the telephone can be turned into a full-time job. Phone aficionados were once only able to find jobs working for phone companies as operators or at switchboards. While these jobs still exist, more positions now exist for telemarketers, catalog order takers, customer service representatives, and answering-service employees. All of these jobs have one thing in common—nearly nonstop phone talking. Furthermore, there is a very high demand for people to fill these jobs.

Teachers, Doctors, Lawyers, Politicians, and Clerics

The talking professions have three things in common: they are careers that involve a considerable amount of talking, require specialized knowledge, and often involve long, intensive academic preparation. At the same time, if you choose a career in teaching, medicine, law, politics, or religion, the impact of what you say on the job can play a very significant role in the lives of others. Just think of the effect that teachers have already had on your life, the role lawyers could play in winning or losing a case for you, and the importance of your doctors asking the right questions to make a lifesaving diagnosis of an ailment, and you can easily understand the importance of talking in these professions.

Advice Givers

If your desire to find a profession in which you can talk a lot is coupled with a longing to help others, you should investigate a career providing advice to others. Advice givers are psychologists, psychiatrists, counselors, and social workers. For these careers, you will need to be an empathetic person who can listen as well as talk, and you will usually need to be willing to earn a master's degree. These careers give you the opportunity to help people make important decisions about their lives or get back on track if they are having problems.

Government Spokespeople

The government is the largest single employer in the United States, so it makes sense that there are a great number of jobs that let you talk all day on the national, state, and local levels. Of course, many of these jobs are the same ones you would find with other employers: telephone operators, receptionists, human resources people, lawyers, and dispatchers, to name just a few. Some jobs, however, are only found with the government. You could be a recruiter convincing young people to serve in today's volunteer army. Or you might be a press secretary telling the press and public what an elected official or governmental unit is doing. Then there are all the jobs working behind the counter handling people's needs, from getting a marriage license to obtaining a driver's license.

Travel, Tourism, and Hospitality Talkers

Choose to work in travel, tourism, or hospitality, and you have chosen a job that lets you talk while helping others have a good time. After all, people go to restaurants and hotels, take trips, and sightsee because they want to enjoy themselves. If you are a skilled waitperson, restaurant host, travel agent, reservationist, flight attendant, or tour guide, what you say on the job can add a great deal to other people's enjoyment. It's far more fun for people to take a trip around Manhattan or visit Mammoth Cave National Park with a knowledgeable guide who is a great speaker—mixing facts with humor. And people want to deal with reservationists and travel agents who can determine their needs and then provide the required services.

One of the greatest benefits of a career in travel, tourism, or hospitality is that this is the fastest-growing industry in the world, so there are many jobs available. Also, it is possible to climb the career ladder quickly from an entry-level position.

More Jobs for Talkative Types

Wherever you find people, there will be jobs for talkative types. The easiest way for talkative types to find one of these jobs—from auctioneer to hairstylist to railroad conductor—is by observation. If you are in a shopping mall, look at who's talking. Do the same thing when you are on trips, working part-time, or eating in a restaurant. You can easily discover more jobs for chatty types by simply talking to friends, relatives, and acquaintances about their jobs.

Job Qualifications

While there is an abundance of jobs for talkative types, it isn't enough to just be chatty. You must also have something to say and then say it in a way that others can understand. Quite often, this means getting specialized training or academic degrees. In addition, you must truly enjoy conversing with people, whether you are negotiating a contract, mediating a dispute, giving advice, or selling a product. If you want to learn even more about careers for talkative types, contact some of the organizations listed in the Appendix for helpful career information.

CHAPTER TWO

Lights! Camera! Action!

Glamour Talkers in the Limelight

D ay after day, millions of us watch and listen to fabulous talkers in the limelight. We start our mornings with Diane Sawyer or Matt Lauer giving us the news and sharing stories of interest. Oprah Winfrey, Regis and Kelly, and Dr. Phil entertain us throughout the day. Larry King and Rush Limbaugh challenge us with their opinions. David Letterman and Jay Leno help us end the day with humor.

These stars of radio and television have reached the heights of stardom because they have the gift of gab. Right behind them, waiting in the wings to gain national prominence, are thousands of others with the same gift who talk to us every day on local radio and television stations.

Of course, you don't have to be a talk show or morning show host to have a job that involves nonstop chatter in the public eye. There are jobs for those who present the news (Charles Gibson), weather (Al Roker), sports (John Madden), entertainment (Mary Hart), and special information segments on radio and television.

You can also find a job in the limelight as a comedian making people laugh in clubs, stage shows, radio, and television. Some very eloquent people even earn their living as speakers.

Preparing for a Radio or Television Job

Preparation for entering one of these glamorous careers is just up a talkative type's alley. You simply have to talk as much as you can to gain experience that will result in performing successfully in the public eye. In school, this can mean participating in debate and theatrical productions as well as gaining valuable experience at campus radio or TV facilities. Another possibility is on-the-job training in the form of an internship or apprentice program at a local station.

First jobs most likely will not be on-air jobs. Many television personalities, including Johnny Carson, got started as ushers for TV shows. Other radio and television performers have had first jobs as receptionists, production assistants, writers, researchers, or anything that would let them get a foot in the door. Their on-the-air careers often began as remote reporters, announcers, or interviewers. A beginner's best chance for landing an on-air job is at a small radio or television station. Jane Pauley, for example, began at a small TV station in Indiana.

Low Pay and Intense Competition

Salaries in radio and television vary widely. While megastars such as Rush Limbaugh, David Letterman, Regis Philbin, and Oprah Winfrey earn millions, pay is low for many others, especially beginners. In general, salaries are higher in television than in radio, higher in larger markets than in smaller ones, and higher in commercial than in public broadcasting.

The average salary for reporters and correspondents in radio and television is $34,000 per year. Television news anchors might earn from about $25,000 in a small market to more than $200,000 in the largest markets. Overall, sportscasters average about $39,000 in radio and $49,000 in television.

Competition for jobs in radio and television is always intense because so many people are attracted to this glamorous industry. There are always far more job seekers than jobs. Most openings arise from people leaving the profession—often because they were unable to advance to better-paying jobs. Because competition for ratings is always keen, especially in major metropolitan areas, large radio and television stations continue to seek individuals who have proven that they can attract and retain a large audience.

. . . .

Radio—a Talker's Dream Career

Long before television was popular, people gathered around their radios every evening. They listened to "One Man's Family," "The Jack Benny Program," and "Inner Sanctum Mysteries" for entertainment. Lowell Thomas, Edward R. Murrow, and other famous commentators kept them in touch with what was going on in the world. President Franklin Delano Roosevelt used the medium to host his weekly fireside chats. This golden age of radio ended when television took over many of these roles.

Radio did not roll over and play dead. Instead, radio changed its format. All-talk, all-news, and all-music stations emerged, as well as stations with formats designed to attract a particular audience. Soon radio had captured more listeners than ever before. In fact, homes today have a far greater number of radios than television sets.

Many jobs in radio are perfect for verbose people. You could exercise your proclivity for chatter and dispense advice on a talk show dealing with medical matters, food, cars, investments, or a wide range of other subjects. Or you could chat with individuals who call a program to interact with the host and other listeners. Radio is not just talk shows or disc jockeys playing music. There are a great number of jobs for people who report the news, sports, weather, and traffic.

The Barbara Simpson Program

Barbara Simpson can talk about anything, ad-lib forever, and think on her feet. And this is exactly what she does every Saturday and Sunday on her 4:00 to 7:00 P.M. radio talk program on KSFO in San Francisco as well as on frequent weekday fill-in appearances. Barbara, an expert on political and social issues, begins her program by chatting with her live audience about a variety of topics, ranging from something that is disturbing her to controversial items in the day's news. Because her program follows a taped talk show, what she says must be interesting and challenging, even feisty, to get listeners to call in. Once the calls start coming, Barbara never knows what her audience will talk about. It could be one or more of the topics that she mentioned or a casual remark from a listener that captures everyone's interest. Unlike many talk show programs, where callers are screened out, Barbara welcomes both those who agree and those who disagree with her on any subject. By the end of each three-hour program, she and her listeners will have exchanged views on a wide variety of issues.

Preparing for a Talk Show. In order to do a talk show, it is absolutely essential to keep up-to-date with what is happening in the world. Barbara loves this aspect of her job and feels she is really being paid to learn. Each month she looks at approximately fifty-five publications, from *People* to *National Review*. Besides perusing six newspapers daily, she reads the news coming over the wire at the station. Wherever she is, the radio is always on so she can listen to other talk shows and the news. Barbara gets ideas for her program everywhere. A book review in a newspaper about a new book on astronomy may inspire her to invite its author to appear on the program. The mention of food contamination in a news report may give her an idea for a topic to discuss.

Barbara's Media Resume. For the past twenty years, Barbara has been a well-known radio and television newsperson in the San Francisco Bay Area and Los Angeles. For part of her career, she worked at the same time in both radio and television. Barbara's career as a radio talk show host began in Los Angeles on KABC. Since then, she has hosted talk shows in Sacramento and San Francisco and has written and reported medical, legal, consumer, and environmental commentaries for Los Angeles, San Francisco, and national radio stations. Barbara was also the producer, writer, and reporter of "Earth Journal," which aired nationally on CBS radio for five years.

Barbara's television resume is equally impressive. She has been a news anchor in San Francisco and Los Angeles. During that time, she received two Emmy Awards as an anchor and saw the investigative unit, "On Target," which she originated, nominated for an Emmy. She has also produced, reported, and hosted a bimonthly news/interview program.

A Broad Background. There is no one route to becoming a successful talk show host. Barbara has a bachelor's degree in merchandising and a master's degree in textiles and clothing with a minor in communications. Besides her work in the broadcasting media, she has been a college associate professor of textiles and clothing; worked in public relations and marketing; written newspaper columns on social and political issues; helped design and coordinate a worldwide petition campaign; served as public relations director of the Cousteau Society; done media consulting for politics, business, and the environment through her own company; and starred in theatrical and television productions. Many of these different jobs have overlapped.

Career Advice and Insights. For a career in talk radio, Barbara believes that you have to be insatiably curious, extremely persistent, and very knowledgeable. She recommends a degree in traditional liberal arts with an emphasis in history because it gives you the knowledge needed to measure today's events by how they fit into the past. Barbara also advocates finding an internship so you can evaluate whether or not a career in broadcasting is really right for you.

According to Barbara, talk radio—in fact, all radio—is a little bit of glamour, a whole lot of work, and little pay, especially for beginners. It is also a cutthroat business in which you need to have a thick skin and a strong ego to survive. Barbara, however, admits to loving everything about this career despite its negatives because it's challenging, varied, and fun.

Afternoon Anchor of an All-News Station

The San Francisco Bay Area is one of the most traffic-congested places in the country. On all-news station KCBS, Mike Pulsipher and Patti Reising anchor the news for the afternoon drive between 2:00 and 7:00 P.M., Monday through Friday. They work together so smoothly that Mike often begins, "Some of the stories we are following," and Patti lists the stories. Although much of their time is spent reading the news, there is also considerable ad-libbing and chitchatting between the anchors. For example, after Patti recently read news of the death of a disc jockey, Mike shared some of his personal memories of working with this man.

Before the program begins, Mike and Patti write the script for the news on the first hour. Other reporters who will be on the program help by dictating the leads into their stories. The script for the rest of the news program is handled by other writers. When they go on the air, the coanchors have a lineup detailing what will happen each hour. Their news reporting is interspersed by other reporters giving frequent news, traffic, weather, and sports updates.

Mike's Career Path. Before he even started college, Mike had attended a radio school and learned a few basics of broadcasting. A friend told him of an upcoming vacancy at a Sacramento station, and he got the job as an announcer doing a bit of everything. Throughout his years in college, he kept this job and has been in radio ever since at stations in Los Angeles, New York, and San Francisco. Although he no longer travels in his present job, in the past he has flown on Air Force One with President Bush and covered many political conventions as well as the first Reagan-Gorbachev summit. Mike is very happy with his career, especially its fast pace and the fact that news is new every day.

Career Advice. If you are not a talkative person with the gift of gab, you can do several things to acquire this skill. Future news reporters can tape themselves reading the newspaper aloud and then listen to the tapes. Future disc jockeys can practice their ad-libbing in the same way.

A Traffic and Weather Reporter

By the age of five, Ron Lyons was imitating radio announcers. When he was a junior in high school, he became a jack-of-all-trades at a radio station, and he has been in radio ever since. Today, he is the traffic and weather reporter on the same station as Mike Pulsipher, doing the early morning commute program from 5:00 to 10:00 A.M. In this job, Ron delivers the information that helps make the morning commute more tolerable to all the drivers getting into their cars at the crack of dawn so they can arrive at work on time.

Ron's workstation is a small booth with two computers—one gives information from the California Highway Patrol (CHP) on traffic stalls and accidents, and the other from a service combines traffic information from the CHP and cell phones. Each morning the station also has four or five aircraft viewing the traffic. Using information from all of these sources, Ron tries to find the significant traffic bottlenecks in order to give a one-minute traffic report every ten minutes. During this brief interval, he describes traffic problems and goes to several of the aircraft for on-air updates. Then at the end of the traffic segment, he gives a ten- or twenty-second weather report. This work is very intense and challenging as a lot of split-second decisions have to be made. Furthermore, everything that Ron says is ad-libbed—he really has to think on his feet.

Ron's workday is not over when the program ends. He then spends one and a half to two hours or more preparing station commercials and promotions. The material is usually written, but he has to read it and add the music. Ron uses a state-of-the-art digital editor to do this. Each commercial and promotion takes from ten or fifteen minutes to an hour to complete. He typically does two or three pieces but may do as many as six.

Ron's Background. Ron's career began as the golden days of radio, with its dramas, were ending, and it has spanned more than forty years. At times, he has dabbled in television, but he is really a radio person. Wherever he has worked, he has had to do a variety of things to survive—news, weather, and traffic. Young people entering the profession should expect to do this, too. They should also be ready to face one of the downsides of this profession, which is being fired from a job. This has happened to Ron twice in his long career.

Although Ron is now doing traffic and weather, for much of his career he was a disc jockey. In fact, he was one of the first to play a Beatles record on the air. He has also been a program director and a news anchor.

Career Advice. If you want a career in radio, Ron says to be prepared for a lot of rejection when seeking a job because competition is so keen. He anticipates that twenty to thirty people would be competing for his job if he left it. His advice is to learn all you can about computers and all kinds of multimedia to prepare for a career. Ron believes that the possibility of making a lot of money in radio is always there, but there is little likelihood of most aspiring radio careerists doing so.

Television—Talented Talkers on Screen

In the United States, television sets are found in more than 98 percent of the homes, and these sets are on for an average of more than six hours a day. From the crack of dawn until late at night, there are many households where the television set or sets are rarely off. What is significant to the job seeker is the huge number of programs on which people are talking. The possibilities range from being the anchor of a news program, like Brian Williams, to a reporter who adds commentary from the studio, community, or anywhere in the world. You could interview celebrities, as Barbara Walters does, or be a football commentator like Terry Bradshaw. Or you could be at a small TV station giving the forecast for tomorrow's weather or on public television hosting a talk show. With the recent proliferation of channels, there are more jobs than ever before in television for those seeking careers that require considerable talking.

Furthermore, there is a greater variety in the types of programs offered on different channels. In addition to the traditional network channels, you could find a career on an educational, all-news, history, travel, or sports channel or on a shopping channel selling all kinds of goods.

NBC News Anchor in a Major Market

It had been twelve years since anyone interviewed Mother Teresa for American television when Anne Ryder of Channel 13 in Indianapolis arrived in Calcutta. After working for several days as a volunteer, Anne gained the famed humanitarian's trust and was granted a forty-five-minute sit-down interview with her. It turned out to be very significant as it was the last interview that Mother Teresa gave.

When you are the news anchor of 5:00, 6:00, and 11:00 P.M. broadcasts Monday through Friday, your job is so much more than reading the news from a teleprompter. Anne travels around the world to report on what is happening, whether it is a shuttle liftoff or reports of a religious miracle in a war-torn village in Bosnia. She also has to be ready to respond to breaking news and stay on camera without a script, describing a situation as it happens, whether it's a hostage crisis at a restaurant or a search for an assailant who shot a policewoman. Additionally, Anne is the reporter and researcher for "Hope to Tell," a once-a-week news segment with inspirational stories of hope and faith, which has given her the opportunity to talk to many present-day Good Samaritans.

Career Advice. Anne advises those who wish to follow in her footsteps to begin their careers in a small market and learn all aspects of reporting there, from shooting videotapes to producing a newscast. She began her own career in a small television station in Lafayette, Indiana, after graduating from the University of Missouri with a degree in journalism. Her next step up the career ladder was to Terre Haute, Indiana, where she was a general-assignment reporter. Anne handled everything at this station, from the weather to weekend anchor to main anchor. Then Anne moved to WTHR in Indianapolis, where she started as a community affairs weekend producer and then became a consumer reporter. This was followed by stints as weekend coanchor and sunrise coanchor until she became the evening anchor. In 2004 Anne left the WTHR anchor desk to "achieve a better balance between work and family." She still contributes special reports to the news broadcasts.

Anne credits much of her verbal facility to acquiring the habit of reading a lot as a child. This helped her develop both the writing and speaking skills that are prerequisites for being a successful news anchor.

....

Comedians

Their witty words make you laugh, whether you see them on television or on stage in Las Vegas, Atlantic City, or your hometown. Comedians are the chattiest people in the entertainment world. They are literally nonstop talkers for the length of their shows, pausing only long enough for the audience to laugh at their best jokes or humorous remarks. No one succeeds in this career without a willingness to spend years in small clubs refining his or her delivery and developing good material. We all are acquainted with well-known comedians, such as Jerry Seinfeld, Ellen DeGeneres, George Lopez, Drew Carey, and Rosie O'Donnell. There are many more comedians in small clubs and comedy stores honing their skills and waiting for the big break. Most will never gain national prominence; however, many will have long careers presenting their material in small clubs and lounge acts; opening shows for stars; acting in stage shows, movies, and television; and bringing their humor to convention goers and other groups.

David Letterman

If you are going to become a comedian, you need to be patient. After a stint as a weathercaster in the Midwest, David Letterman went to Los Angeles, where he worked the stand-up comedy circuit while writing material for sitcoms. His big break came after appearances on "The Tonight Show" led to his becoming a regular guest host for Johnny Carson. Then he was given his own daytime show, which lasted only a few months. However, executives at NBC were impressed with his work, and he was given the opportunity to start the late-night show that has brought him so much fame—first on NBC, then on CBS.

Rosie O'Donnell

Like this well-known comedian, you can begin to hone your comedic skills in high school. Rosie was just sixteen years old when she gave such a smashing performance as a Gilda Radner character in a school show that she was encouraged to try stand-up comedy. For the next four years, she introduced comedians at shows and learned from observing their acts. Then at age twenty, Rosie went out on the road and traveled the club circuit on the East Coast. Very few women were doing comedy then; the wages were very low, and the conditions backstage were appalling.

Nevertheless, Rosie kept working and succeeded as a comedian, winning the "Star Search" talent competition several times. After a short stint on a TV sitcom, she produced and hosted "Stand-Up Spotlight" on television. Then her movie career took off as she was in several blockbuster movies: *A League of Their Own*, *Sleepless in Seattle*, and *The Flintstones*. Rosie is a champion chatterer and created her own TV talk show, "The Rosie O'Donnell Show," which ran from 1996 to 2002.

. . . .

Speakers

Former presidents of the United States often become speakers, as do sports greats, syndicated columnists, authors, entertainers, and military heroes. You don't, however, have to be a well-known person to have a career as a speaker. What you must be is a fabulous speaker. Then you can find jobs as a master of ceremonies, keynote speaker, lecturer, or conference speaker. Typically, a speaker's bureau finds jobs for you and handles the arrangements for your speaking engagements. While well-known speakers like Bill Cosby can command as much as $120,000 for a single speech, speakers who address corporate audiences can earn between $4,000 and $100,000 per speech. Even being a speaker in the small education niche talking to students, parents, and educators can mean fees between $500 and $3,000 per speech.

Entering This Profession

You are not going to enter this field without experience. Audiences want to hear polished speakers. Typically, this means four to five years of speaking to groups. You can begin to get this experience in school by working as a student leader. Then you can refine your skills in front of small community groups. Speaking well is just one facet of creating a career as a speaker. You need to have something worthwhile to say. There are many choices, such as motivational messages, uplifting speeches, informational speeches, amusing stories, instructional lectures, travelogues, and comedy. For example, there are speakers who are making a living talking about investing in stocks, getting the best health care, the consequences of being a gang member, traveling through Turkey, stopping smoking, motivating assembly-line workers, overcoming dyslexia, or selling a particular product. Once you have gained credentials as a speaker, you can have a professional audio or video tape made of one of your speeches and send it to prospective clients or to speaker's bureaus that may want to add you to the list of available speakers.

Talking Can Be Glamorous

While you may envision millions of people hanging onto every word you say on radio or television, be aware of the fact that thousands of other people share your dream. It is not easy to break into the broadcasting field. Nor is it easy to become a popular comedian or a sought-after speaker. There are no guarantees of good salaries, short hours, or pressure-free days. Like all careers, those that involve speaking in the limelight also involve considerable drudgery. However, these careers are exciting, and most people who have them truly enjoy them.

CHAPTER THREE

The Great Persuaders

Sales Talkers

Salespeople have a way with words that is legendary. These chatterboxes of the business world never truly accept a no answer from a prospective customer. You find them traveling to companies to sell products or services, behind the counters or out on the floor selling merchandise in stores, or on the road selling homes, insurance, stocks, or bonds to the public. Salespeople are the ones who can shoot the breeze with anyone, from the next-door neighbor to a farmer on the prairie to the sophisticated owner of a major business. Whether it is a new house, car, perfume, stock, or insurance, if the ears hear the right verbal pitch, the hands reach for the money and buy. Whenever people buy anything, there is usually a salesperson with the gift of gab involved in the transaction in some way.

Sales Representatives

Computers, compact discs, and clothing are among the thousands of products bought and sold each day. Sales representatives are an important part of this sales process. They are the persuasive people who sell products to manufacturers, wholesale and retail establishments, government agencies, and other institutions. They may sell fabric to furniture manufacturers, blue jeans to department stores, canned goods to wholesalers, or computers to schools. No matter what type of product they sell, their job is to interest wholesale and retail buyers and purchasing agents in their merchandise and to ensure that any questions or concerns of current clients are addressed.

Depending on where they work, sales representatives have different job titles. Many of those working directly for manufacturers are referred to as manufacturers' representatives, and those employed by wholesalers generally are called sales representatives, while those selling technical products may be called sales engineers. Since these titles are often used interchangeably, we refer to all these salespeople as sales representatives.

What Happens on the Job

Sales representatives spend much of their time traveling to and visiting with prospective buyers and current clients. During sales calls, they discuss the customers' needs and suggest how their merchandise or services can meet those needs. They may show samples or catalogs that describe items their companies stock and inform customers about prices, availability, and how their products can save money and improve productivity.

Because of the vast number of manufacturers and wholesalers selling similar products, sales representatives usually try to emphasize the unique qualities of the products and services offered by their companies—a welcome challenge for their verbal skills. They also take orders and resolve any problems or complaints with the merchandise. They may provide advice to clients on how to increase retail sales, too. Obtaining new accounts is another important part of this job. Sales representatives also analyze sales statistics, prepare reports, and handle administrative duties, such as filing expense account reports, scheduling appointments, and making travel plans.

Although the hours are long and often irregular, most sales representatives have the freedom of determining their own schedules. As a result, they may be able to arrange their appointments so that they can have time off when they want it.

If you take a job as a sales representative, it is important to understand that you will often face competition from other sales representatives selling similar products. There also may be competition with fellow workers if the company has set goals or quotas that representatives are expected to meet. In addition, dealing with different types of people can be demanding.

Earnings

Most sales representatives receive a combination of salary and commission or salary plus bonus. The average yearly salary is more than $45,000.

Training for Sales Representatives

The background needed for sales jobs varies by product line and market. You may not need to be a college graduate if you are thoroughly familiar with a product and you are an effective salesperson who could sell ice in the Arctic Circle. Nevertheless, as job requirements have become more technical and analytical, most firms have placed a greater emphasis on a strong educational background, especially since more college graduates are now available.

Many companies have formal training programs that last up to two years for beginning sales representatives. In some firms, new workers are trained by accompanying more experienced workers on their sales calls. As these workers gain familiarity with the firms' products and clients, they are given increasing responsibility until they are eventually assigned their own territories.

Sales Representative for a Corporation

Tony Abernathy is a sales representative for a computer curriculum corporation. The entire focus of his job is communicating with people. Tony prefers to use the word *communicating* instead of *talking* because communicating is both talking and listening. His job often begins with a needs analysis, which means discussing with the customer what technology may be needed. Then, together, they implement a technology plan and create a system of hardware and software that provides the technology solution for the customer's educational needs. Next, Tony does staff training and development. If he is doing his job right, he is either listening or talking most of the time during his working hours.

Tony's first job was as a sixth-grade teacher; he has taught other grades and been a college GED coordinator as well as a sales representative for a textbook company. Tony has a master's degree in elementary education and has had training in implementing technology to integrate math and science—an excellent background for his present job of helping teachers use technology to enhance learning.

Career Advice. Tony was definitely not at ease getting up in front of others in his college speech class; however, when he became a teacher, he became more comfortable as a speaker. He picked up his verbal skills by studying good speakers and modeling their speech habits, and he advises talkative types to do the same.

Selling Fund-Raising Programs

Rebecca (Becky) Young's job is selling fund-raising programs to organizations such as parent-teacher groups, middle schools, high schools, day-care centers, leagues, churches, and athletic groups. In her present job, she lets her customers do a lot of the talking, and they often talk themselves into buying her program. (Part of the secret of being a successful sales representative is knowing when to talk and when to listen.) After selling a program, whether it is over the phone or in person, Becky coordinates the program. For example, she often gets up in front of students to kick off the program at an assembly. She also collects and sends in orders, delivers the product that is being sold as a fund-raiser, handles any problems, and closes out the accounts.

Becky's background includes teaching in junior and senior high school, selling home interior products, and being a corporate administrator. In every job, she used her verbal skills. Years ago, when she placed second out of sixteen in a magazine sales contest in high school, Becky learned that she had an ability to sell. In the future, Becky probably will stay in some kind of sales work as she wants the freedom to move about and call the shots.

Career Advice. Becky's advice to anyone wanting a career like hers is to get a college degree in business, sales, or communications. She also believes that people skills are really speaking skills and that these skills are the key to advancement and success today.

Textbook/Software Sales Representative

Tony Weber is a textbook/software sales representative for a publishing company. He uses the phone to set up appointments, visits customers to discuss product needs, makes product presentations to individuals and groups, and works in exhibit booths at conferences. Tony has always had a job that involves talking with people. His work background includes restaurant management, teaching, and sales and marketing representative positions. Today, he is a senior account manager, which means he is a sales representative who fully manages his accounts. His educational background—a bachelor's degree in marketing and business education and a master's in business administration—is perfect for his job.

Career Advice. Tony's advice to people wanting to go into sales is to get as much education as possible, work hard, listen, and try to make as many stand-up presentations as possible. He feels that he acquired many of his verbal skills from teaching. Also, he takes advantage of the short conferences his company holds that emphasize speaking skills.

Retail Sales Workers

Millions of dollars are spent each day on all types of merchandise—everything from sweaters and cosmetics to lumber and plumbing supplies. Whether you are buying candy, clothes, or furniture, it is the salespeople in retail stores who help you find what you are looking for. They describe the product features, demonstrate its use, or show you various models and colors. If you want to buy a complex or expensive item like a computer, the salesperson has the special knowledge to explain the unique features of different brands and models, the meaning of the manufacturers' specifications, and the types of software on the machine.

In addition to selling, most retail sales workers, especially those who work in department and apparel stores, make out sales checks, receive cash, charge payments, bag or package purchases, and give change and receipts. The job of salesperson is very important because the retail industry is so very competitive, and customers often form their impressions of a store based on its sales force.

Becoming a Sales Worker

Because there is a high turnover rate in sales positions, it is usually possible to get a job. In fact, in some areas, there is an actual shortage of workers. You will probably not have to meet any formal education requirements to become a sales worker; however, a high school diploma or equivalent is increasingly preferred. In order to handle this job, you need to enjoy working with people and have the tact, patience, and verbal communication skills to deal with difficult customers. You should also have an interest in sales work, a neat appearance, and the ability to communicate clearly and effectively.

If you obtain a sales position in a small store, an experienced employee or the owner will probably instruct you in making out sales checks, handling the cash register, and using solid sales techniques. If you get a job with a large store, your training will be more formal and may include actual classes or at least manuals and videos for you to study. Once your training is completed, you should expect to work for a while under the direction of a more experienced worker.

Selling Cosmetics in a Mall Store

When she was just seventeen years old and still in high school, Melinda Joseph got her first sales job selling cosmetics part-time. The store, which was part of a national chain, sold cosmetics and offered makeovers and skin-care lessons. Before she ever worked with a customer, Melinda received extensive training from the store owners for about three weeks. She also had to study product manuals so she would know what ingredients were in the cosmetics sold in the store and which ones worked best on different skin types. The company owners showed her how to do makeovers and give skin-care lessons to customers. In addition, Melinda received training in the company's five-step sales procedures, which worked so well she used them in future sales jobs. This included learning to greet customers and determining what products they needed by asking the right questions. Melinda also learned how to close sales right after she demonstrated each product.

Melinda, a very personable individual who can shoot the breeze with anyone, was a very successful salesperson. Almost every customer she waited on bought something. When she did a makeover, she typically sold at least six products. Following company procedures, she created a file for each customer, followed each sale with a personal call or note, and called customers to let them know about free gift offers. In the three and a half years that she worked at this store, Melinda developed a group of loyal, repeat customers.

Melinda enjoyed this sales job because she liked talking to the customers and being able to help them use cosmetics effectively. It also gave her an opportunity to be creative in choosing the right cosmetics for each customer. An additional benefit of this job was the excellent pay. Melinda received both an hourly wage and a sales bonus, which allowed her to earn from $11 to $12 per hour.

On this job, Melinda discovered that she truly loved sales work. While she was still in college, her experience at the store qualified her for another job as counter manager for a cosmetics line at a department store. After college, she became a cosmetics sales manager, supervising fifteen employees. Today, she is the manager of the home furnishings and children's apparel departments of a large department store where the only drawback is that she rarely has the opportunity to get back on the floor and sell.

Selling Casual Clothing

Different stores present different opportunities for salespeople. Andrea Pullen saw an ad in the window of a store selling casual clothing for men and women and applied for the job. She had three interviews before she got the job. In each interview, she was given hypothetical situations and asked how she would handle them. During her first day on the job, Andrea saw a video to acquaint her with the history of the store, which was part of a large national chain. Then a supervisor walked her around the store, showing her where everything was and how to fold shirts and hang pants. Then she was out on her own, approaching customers and asking if she could help them. At first, she only helped customers select clothing. Then she learned how to handle the cash register under the direction of other salespeople. Because she was friendly and seemed to have a knack for working with customers, Andrea did not receive any additional direction from her supervisor. When salespeople in the store had problems, the supervisor would draw them aside and make suggestions.

While Andrea enjoyed this job and had many repeat customers, she did not earn as much money as Melinda because she only received an hourly wage. In addition, Andrea worked long hours—sometimes until midnight, while she and the other salespeople folded clothes or changed displays after the store closed at night.

Cashiers—Register Sales

Supermarkets, department stores, drugstores, gasoline service stations, movie theaters, and many other businesses hire cashiers to register the sale of their merchandise. If you get a job as a cashier, you will total bills, receive money, make change, fill out charge forms, and give receipts while you exchange friendly chitchat with customers. Depending on where you work, you may also serve as the information center of the store, answering questions about where things are located and services the store provides. And you probably will handle returns and exchanges. Although cashiers traditionally have rung up purchases manually using a cash register, many now just pass products over scanners.

Jobs as cashiers are typically entry-level positions requiring little or no previous work experience and no specific educational background. They offer a good opportunity to learn an employer's business and can serve as stepping-stones to other positions, including sales worker.

There is almost always an opportunity to get a job as a cashier as they are needed in businesses of all types. Cashiers' earnings vary from minimum wage to several times that amount, especially in areas where there is intense competition for workers.

Drugstore Sales

Janet Notch has two jobs, as do so many people today. She teaches mentally handicapped children in the public schools and works a total of twenty hours a week as a cashier at a drugstore. Janet definitely enjoys being able to converse with adults in her job at the drugstore after spending all day with five children—only one of whom speaks. Even though she is tired at times from holding two jobs, she makes an effort to interact with every customer, whether she is ringing up a sale, handling an exchange, or answering questions about the store.

Janet feels that talking is an intrinsic part of her job as it helps people relax a bit as they wait in line. Most people enjoy the bantering, and it helps them realize that their turn will be coming up soon. Also, many older people don't have many people to talk with and want this interaction. And most parents, she has discovered, enjoy it when you include their children in the conversation. Talking to the children also distracts them when they are tired and crying, which parents appreciate. By trying to give customers a good experience in the store, Janet encourages people to return to the store for future purchases.

In high school Janet took an aptitude test to find out what careers would be good choices for her. The results were teaching, sales, and acting. As a teacher, she really has to be an actress to keep the children interested in the activities, so, overall, her career choices are most appropriate for her personality.

Career Advice. Janet advises that anyone planning to go into sales must be friendly. Customers will then pick you out and get in your line; management will then notice, and you will definitely get more raises than the grumpy clerk!

Real Estate Agents

The purchase or sale of a home or an investment property is not only one of the most important financial events in peoples' lives, but one of the most complex transactions as well. For this reason, most people seek the expert help of real estate agents, who have a thorough knowledge of the market in their communities, are familiar with local zoning and tax laws, and know where to obtain financing.

The sales process absolutely requires people who have the gift of gab. It begins when the real estate agents meet with clients to get a feeling for the type of home or property they would like and can afford. Agents must use their well-honed verbal skills to get this information. Then agents often use computers to generate lists of properties that are appropriate for their clients. The next step is to take the clients to see some of the properties. Experienced agents tailor their discussions of properties to the individuals. For example, a home may be described to a young family as close to schools but to a retired couple as close to public transportation. Typically, clients view many properties and have several discussions with their real estate agents before making a decision to buy. Then the agent follows the clients' instructions in negotiating to get the best possible price.

When real estate agents sell properties, there is just as much talking. Agents must discuss with the property owners how to present the property in the best possible way and work together to set a sales price. Also, agents help with negotiations once buyers are found.

Preparing to Become a Real Estate Agent

While you do not need to have a college education to become a realtor, you do need to hold a state license, which typically requires completing between thirty and ninety hours of classroom instruction and passing a comprehensive written test. Beginners usually learn the practical aspects of the job, including the use of computers, under the direction of an experienced agent. Some larger companies have formal training programs for new agents.

Earnings

Turnover in the real estate industry is high, so it is usually not too difficult to get a job as a realtor unless the economy is in a downturn. Salaried real estate sales agents earned an average of $35,600 per year. Commissions on sales are the main source of earnings, as few real estate agents receive a salary. The rate of commission varies according to the type of property and its value; the percentage paid on the sale of farm and commercial properties or unimproved land is usually higher than that paid for the sale of a home.

A Real Estate Agent

As a real estate agent, Nancy Johnson does most of her talking with buyers while they are in her car riding around looking at properties. She also does a lot of talking on the phone because she is constantly updating sellers about what people thought of their properties. Nancy also talks with cooperating real estate agents when a property is being bought or sold. She has always enjoyed talking and likes the give and take of people opening up and sharing who they are and what they are about so she can figure out what type of house they are looking for.

When Nancy and her family moved to a new state, she had no network of friends or business associates upon which she could begin to build a real estate career, so she started hosting open houses on weekends and met many young couples who were the same age as her own children. Many of these couples have kept Nancy as their real estate agent through the years.

Nancy was older when she started this career, just as many realtors are, and was able to draw upon past work experiences to succeed. Dealing with parents and children as an elementary school teacher helped her learn patience, tact, and compassion. A job as a receptionist was helpful because she talked to so many people. Nancy believes that her college education gave her the background she needs to talk to her clients who are college graduates. Although she took real estate classes in order to get her license, she feels that the training she got from the real estate company where she works was more helpful.

Career Views. Although this is a perfect career for Nancy, it does have downsides, especially for young people with families. For example, you could be leaving town for a vacation when your beeper goes off, forcing you to turn back because you have an offer on a house. And if you try to sell twenty houses in a year, your phone will be ringing at eleven o'clock at night, and you will be doing paperwork continually. Furthermore, you can't take your children with you to show a house, and you definitely need to have a spouse who understands that you often need to work nights and weekends.

Insurance Agents and Brokers

Most people purchase insurance at some time in their lives to provide protection against loss. In fact, many states require car owners to purchase insurance, and most of us have or want to have health insurance. The professionals who help individuals and businesses select the policies that provide the best insurance protection for their cars and health—as well as for their lives, jewelry, personal valuables, furniture, household items, businesses, and other properties—are known as insurance agents and brokers. Agents may work for one company or as independent agents selling for several insurance companies, while brokers do not work for one company but place insurance policies for their clients with the company that offers the best rate and coverage for their situations.

If you want to be an insurance agent or broker, you need to be enthusiastic, outgoing, self-confident, disciplined, hardworking, and able to communicate effectively. Because personality traits, including the gift of gab, are so important in selling insurance, some companies even give prospective employees personality tests to make sure that they have a "salesperson" personality. You probably need to be a college graduate to be hired as an insurance agent or broker; few high school graduates are chosen unless they have proven sales ability. Companies particularly like graduates who majored in business or economics because an understanding of accounting, tax laws, and economic conditions is helpful in selling insurance.

Employment of insurance agents and brokers is expected to grow more slowly than most other occupations. Most job openings will arise from the need to replace agents and brokers who leave the occupation. Furthermore, selling insurance is a very competitive business, and many beginners find it difficult to establish a sufficiently large clientele and may eventually leave for other jobs.

Earnings

The average earnings of salaried insurance sales workers are more than $41,700 a year. Most independent agents only earn sales commissions.

All Sales Jobs Require Talkative People

There is absolutely no way to sell clothes, computers, cars, insurance, or the thousands of items people buy every day without having the gift of gab. People want to know about the products and services they are buying, whether it is a desk, refrigerator, or insurance policy. They want advice from salespeople: Are these glasses right for me? Which car has the highest safety rating? What is a fair price for this house?

Even though we can now buy many items through catalogs and online through the Internet, there will always be a need for the special help only salespeople can offer. Plus, good salespeople can usually find a job in the very large field of sales.

CHAPTER FOUR

Success!

Talkers in Businesses and Other Organizations

> **HELP WANTED:** Local business needs an articulate person capable of conferring, negotiating, discussing, and speaking convincingly with others.

If the preceeding ad caught your attention, then you may want to use your gift of gab to do what you like to do best—spend most of your time talking. Within businesses and other organizations, your speaking skills play an important role in just about any job you hold. There are a few opportunities when the people with whom you talk are not fellow workers but instead potential clients or customers. You are, in a sense, a voice for your company or organization, encouraging people to buy products or services or to think highly of your workplace. Or you could be an outside contractor performing these same services.

In earlier chapters, we have described such jobs as sales worker, telephone operator, and customer service representative—all jobs for talkers in businesses and organizations. In this chapter, we add to the list—jobs in reception, marketing, public relations, and human resources, all of which are perfect for talkative types. What you say in all these jobs can have a definite influence on the success of your company or organization.

....

Reception

The image of a business or organization is important. Are people eager to accommodate you? Are you greeted warmly when you call or visit? Are the people with whom you deal competent? No one likes to be associated with a business or organization whose employees are cold, hostile, and remote. It is the receptionist sitting close to the entry who makes the first impression many people have of a business or organization. The traditional duties of a receptionist are to greet visitors, answer general questions, and direct or announce visitors to the individuals they wish to see. Receptionists may also have a security function—monitoring the access of visitors and determining who belongs and who does not.

The day-to-day duties of receptionists vary depending upon where they work. As a receptionist in a hospital or a doctor's or dentist's office, you might greet patients, obtain financial and personal information, and direct patients to the proper waiting rooms. If you work in a hair or beauty salon, you would arrange appointments, direct customers to hairstylists, and serve as cashier, taking payments for services and products. In factories, newspapers, large corporations, and government offices, you might also provide visitors with identification cards and arrange for escorts to take them to the proper offices.

In addition, at many of these workplaces, you could find yourself answering telephones and routing calls to the appropriate individuals. When receptionists are not busy with callers or visitors, they often perform a variety of secretarial duties, including opening and sorting mail, collecting and distributing packages, making fax transmittals, updating appointment calendars, preparing travel vouchers, and doing simple bookkeeping, typing, and filing. Today, more and more receptionists find themselves using personal computers to handle their jobs. No matter how many other tasks receptionists have, their major role remains to greet visitors.

Getting and Handling a Receptionist Job

It should be easy to get a job as a receptionist well beyond the first decade of the twenty-first century because so many businesses that require receptionists are growing rapidly, such as doctors' and dentists' offices, hospitals, law firms, temporary help agencies, and consulting firms. In addition to new openings, many vacancies occur as receptionists leave the job to seek better pay or advancement. Being a receptionist can provide a springboard to many other jobs at a company or organization.

Receptionists usually learn how to handle their positions on the job. Some businesses and organizations, however, prefer job applicants to have had some formal office education or training.

Earnings

Most receptionists work full-time; only about three out of ten work part-time. Most receptionists hold positions in service industries, especially in health services, which includes doctors' and dentists' offices, hospitals, nursing homes, urgent care centers, surgical centers, and clinics. The average earnings for all receptionists are more than $21,000 a year, with those working for the federal government averaging more than $29,000 a year. Very few receptionists belong to unions.

Dental Receptionist

When Diana Davis was in sixth grade, she was already a confirmed chatterer. One day, when she was talking to a classmate, the teacher stopped her lecture, went over to Diana's desk, and said, "I swear if I put a statue next to you, you'd talk to it." Diana believes that this was true then and is true now. She has always enjoyed talking, and her job as a receptionist in a dentist's office lets her spend much of her day chatting with patients.

When it comes to dentistry, Diana knows what she is talking about because she was a chair-side assistant before she became a receptionist. This enables her to talk knowledgeably with clients about their dental problems. In addition, she has taken many seminars on dealing with various aspects of her job as well as the different personalities of the patients. She has also learned how to communicate effectively with patients by studying their reactions to what she says. Part of her role is to put them at ease, knowing they may be facing an uncomfortable situation.

Diana works full-time as a receptionist. She arrives at the office at 8:00 A.M. and is busy turning on the computer, calling the answering service for messages, organizing patients' charts, and unlocking file cabinets before the first patients arrive. During the day, her time is spent greeting patients, answering the phone, making new and follow-up appointments, handling financial arrangements, discussing treatment plans, and dealing with the collection of insurance. She is also in daily contact with the offices of dental specialists because often patients need to be referred to them. In addition, she has the responsibility of calling patients to remind them of scheduled appointments or to schedule appointments for checkups. Her busy day ends at 5:00 P.M. For Diana, being a dental receptionist is an exceptionally enjoyable career because it lets her communicate with people and use her knowledge of dentistry.

Receptionist at an Architectural Firm

Eve Anderson is a receptionist for a large architectural firm that specializes in designing sports and entertainment facilities. The firm employs approximately sixty people who constantly meet with clients and vendors. It is her job to greet these visitors and make them feel welcome and important to the firm. Not only does Eve talk with visitors, she also tries to make them as comfortable as possible by offering them water, coffee, or soft drinks. She may even provide special help for them by typing or faxing documents. To be an effective receptionist, she has learned to recognize frequent visitors so she doesn't have to ask them their names each visit. Eve also answers the phone and routes calls to the appropriate employees.

When you speak with Eve, you immediately realize how friendly, upbeat, and welcoming she sounds. It is these qualities that helped her obtain her first job as a receptionist. Eve was working as a temporary secretary at a law firm and was asked to fill in for the receptionist while she took a lunch break. Several clients called back the next day and told the attorneys how great she was, and a temporary assignment turned into a full-time job for Eve, who has now been a receptionist for the past ten years. Before becoming a receptionist, Eve worked in retail after high school and went from sales associate to manager of a store. It was this position that taught her how to converse effectively with people as she discovered how much help and conversation various customers wanted.

Career Advice. Eve advises young people who are interested in becoming receptionists to try to get as much education as possible and to concentrate on learning proper English. Once you become a receptionist, she believes that your number one goal each day should always be to be polite and courteous to everyone.

Receptionist and Secretary at a Government Agency

In her job as a receptionist and secretary at a state agency, Mary West spends her day talking to people as she helps them find the people with whom they wish to visit. Many of the people who come to her desk are volunteers, and she must match them with the right professional at the agency. To handle this task, Mary has to be well-acquainted with everyone at the agency (new and old employees) as well as their duties. Although she has secretarial responsibilities in this job, the emphasis is definitely on being a receptionist. Mary really likes the contact with people that she has in this job and has discovered she can usually talk grumpy people into a friendlier mood. Mary believes that being a receptionist is an excellent way to get a first job in a company.

....

Marketing

Marketing is a career composed of many different elements. Research determines whether consumers want a product, product development creates the product, advertising promotes the product, sales promotion motivates sales workers, public relations promotes both the company and the product, and distribution and sales get the product to the consumer.

In small firms, all marketing responsibilities may be assumed by the owner or chief executive officer. In large firms, which may offer numerous products and services nationally or even internationally, marketing managers coordinate all marketing activities with the help of managers from different departments.

Preparing to Be a Marketing Manager

There is no one educational background that is appropriate for marketing positions. Many employers prefer a broad liberal arts background, while others want employees to have bachelor's or master's degrees in business administration.

In highly technical industries, such as computer and electronics manufacturing, a bachelor's degree in engineering or computer science combined with a master's degree in business administration is favored. For most marketing positions, familiarity with computerized word processing and database applications is important. Furthermore, the ability to communicate with other managers and the public is vital.

Advancement in marketing can be accelerated by participation in management training programs, which may be offered either in-house or at local colleges and universities. Numerous marketing associations also sponsor management training programs. In addition, certification from a national marketing association based on education and job performance is a sign of achievement or competence in this field.

A Look at Salaries and the Future

The starting salaries for college graduates majoring in marketing average more than $34,000 a year. The median salary of marketing managers is more than $87,000 a year. Many managers also earn bonuses equivalent to 10 percent or more of their salaries. Salary levels vary greatly with the level of responsibility, education, length of service, and the employer's size, location, and industry.

At the present time, jobs in marketing are highly coveted by college graduates. Growth in marketing jobs is expected to be much faster than average in business service industries; however, many manufacturing companies have eliminated marketing departments and outsourced this work to firms specializing in marketing, promotion, and advertising activities.

College Sports Marketer

Can you imagine promoting beach volleyball and college sports? These are just two of the interesting jobs that Tori Engel has enjoyed in marketing. After graduating from college with a degree in economics, she worked as a financial analyst at an investment bank. Two years in this job convinced her that being an analyst involved too much paperwork and too little contact with people. Tori decided she wanted to learn about marketing and promoting events, so she prepared for this new career by taking an internship with a sports marketing firm.

Tori's first assignment was promoting beach volleyball. Each week there would be a tournament in a new city. The promotional work involved nonstop talking. She spoke with the players, with city officials to coordinate the setting up and tearing down of facilities (bleachers, restrooms, and so forth), with sponsors and prospective sponsors, and with the press.

Promoting College Sports. With the internship as experience
on her resume, Tori was able to obtain a job as a marketing coordinator for the sports department of a Pac-Ten school. Initially,
she worked under the sponsorship director. It was her job to deal
with sponsors, which involved finding out how many tickets they
wanted for a game, getting passes for them, and seeing that sponsorship announcements were made over the public address system
at games to get their names in front of alumni and students. Tori
also worked at gaining sponsors so that different youth groups
could attend college games. She was like an ambassador for the
school—getting people to be involved and stay involved. Much of
her work was on the phone; however, during football season she
was often in the press box hosting sponsors. There, Tori chatted
with the sponsors about renewing their sponsorships, getting better tickets, and receiving other benefits. This was decidedly not a
five-day-a-week job as there were sports events at the school every
day. Besides being a skilled communicator, she truly needed to
enjoy sports to handle this job.

After two years as a marketing coordinator, Tori became a marketing manager in charge of several sports. It became her job to
get sponsors, sell large blocks of tickets to groups, talk with the
media, and oversee the placement of ads. She was talking constantly in this job, whether it was to players, potential sponsors,
the media, or coworkers. At meetings, she had to be comfortable
talking to groups—a skill she had acquired through leadership
roles in high school and college.

A New Job. An ad in the newspaper for a marketing director who
was able to work in a chaotic environment and handle a lot of
details caught Tori's attention. Continuing her upward career
path, she applied for the job and became the marketing director at
a large architectural firm specializing in sports and entertainment
facilities. Now she is selling the design and planning talents of her
firm's architects to potential clients. Part of her job is attending

seminars and trade shows, where she talks for eight hours a day about her firm's projects, people, and philosophy.

With each job, including this one, Tori has had to learn the words and phrases associated with the product she markets. For her first job, she had to learn the specific terminology used in beach volleyball; now she has learned the appropriate vocabulary for an architectural firm. A marketing career has given her the opportunity to communicate with people in exciting jobs, which suits her "talkative type" personality.

Project Manager in Marketing

Mary McGowan radiates enthusiasm when you talk to her—an essential quality for being successful in marketing. It was, however, her leadership skills that impressed her employers when she applied for a marketing job at a large telephone company. As a graduate student in English literature, Mary had worked as a residence assistant at a college freshman dormitory and been instrumental in having a Supreme Court justice speak to her group, which demonstrated her initiative. She had also been a head counselor at a summer leadership camp for select high school seniors. Because of her leadership background, the company placed her in its accelerated management program, where her first assignment was as marketing project manager of a group that bought telephone equipment from vendors (manufacturers) and resold it to phone company customers.

In this job, Mary managed a team of eight union-represented employees who took calls from customers wishing to place orders and then called the vendors to order the equipment. When there was a problem with an order, the equipment, or pricing, she stepped in to resolve it. This job also involved considerable travel to meet with customers. For Mary, the most important and rewarding aspect of this job was the coaching, development, and training of her staff. For about two hours each day, she worked with her staff to help them improve anything from telephone skills to processing orders. And once a month she conducted one-on-one, hour-long meetings with each member of the team to discuss his or her career goals and to work on the implementation of a personal career development plan.

According to Mary, building a strong team relationship is an essential component of successful group work. She held weekly staff meetings to discuss particularly difficult assignments—always being sure to end the meetings on a positive note. She also found that planning activities outside of the workplace helped to cement a good team relationship. On this job, Mary spent about 70 percent of her twelve- to fourteen-hour days talking to workers and customers. She also ran trade shows, where she worked alone in a booth talking nonstop to three or four customers at a time.

Preparing for Advancement. Mary was so successful in her work that she received a promotion and a new assignment in which she was totally responsible for the marketing of a $1.2 million revenue-generating program. In the course of her work on the first project, she had further laid the groundwork for this promotion by taking a marketing course that gave her a certificate in marketing. She had also taken a three-day speech course for management to hone her speaking and presentation skills. Mary's career in marketing points out the role that certification and extra courses can play in advancing one's career.

. . . .

Public Relations

It is perfectly clear to most people what doctors, lawyers, and teachers do and why these occupations exist. People are not nearly as sure what a job in "public relations" entails or exactly what "public relations" is. The Public Relations Society of America has formally adopted this definition: "Public relations helps an organization and its publics adapt mutually to each other." An organization's reputation, profitability, and even its continued existence can depend on the degree to which its goals and activities are supported by its targeted "publics." Individuals employed in public relations serve as advocates for businesses, governmental bodies, universities, hospitals, schools, and other organizations and work to build and maintain positive relationships with the public.

The Tasks of Public Relations Specialists

Public relations specialists may work for businesses and other organizations or be employees of public relations firms. Depending on where they work, specialists may handle one or more of these activities:

- telling an organization's story
- promoting the sale of a product
- building positive investor relations by serving as liaison between a company and its shareholders
- lobbying for or against pending legislation
- improving employee relations by coordinating communication between management and employees
- promoting the contribution of funds for worthy causes
- researching attitudes and behaviors of different groups
- organizing and planning community activities

Since the basis of all public relations work is communicating, most specialists have jobs that involve a great deal of talking. They contact media people to get material printed or broadcast. They talk to individuals and groups to keep them aware of what organizations are doing. They spend time on the phone researching the attitudes and concerns of the public and then relate this information to organizations.

Public relations specialists must also cultivate relationships with other professionals. Besides talking, public relations specialists spend time setting up speaking engagements, preparing press releases, researching, making slide and visual presentation materials, planning conventions and meetings, preparing annual reports, and writing proposals for various projects. They may also handle advertising or sales promotion work to support marketing.

Preparing for a Public Relations Career

The best preparation for a career in public relations is to have a college degree coupled with public relations experience, usually gained through an internship. Many beginners major in public relations, journalism, advertising, or communications in college. According to the Public Relations Society of America, the most valuable internships are those involving one or more of the following duties: writing, layout, and editing for external or internal publications, promotional material, and brochures; news gathering; news release and feature writing; research and report writing; preparing local media lists; designing audiovisual presentations; helping to arrange or taking part in special events; and assisting in fund-raising programs.

While in college, students planning to have a career in public relations should join a local chapter of the Public Relations Student Society of America (PRSSA) or the International Association of Business Communicators (IABC) in order to exchange views with public relations specialists in the field and to make contact with professionals who may help them find a full-time job in public relations. The PRSSA has case-study competitions and volunteer programs that give students even more hands-on public relations experience. The organization also sponsors scholarship and internship programs. In preparation for obtaining a job in public relations, it is helpful to build a portfolio of published articles, television or radio programs, and slide presentations to show to prospective employers.

Because communication is so important in this profession, it is vital to build solid speaking skills through such activities as debating, holding leadership positions, participating in theatrical productions, and taking speech classes. You need the ability to make successful face-to-face contact with both individuals and groups. Other important skills or attributes include creativity, imagination, good judgment, sensitivity to other people, decision making, research, planning, and organization. And, of course, as with most professions today, some computer expertise is essential.

The Employment Picture

In recent years, the public relations field has grown enormously as organizations have begun to realize the many ways these specialists can help them. In the future, it is expected that corporate downsizing could limit employment growth with businesses. Employment should, however, increase with public relations firms as organizations hire contractors to provide public relations services rather than support full-time staff. The vast majority of job opportunities should result from the need to replace specialists who leave the profession to take another job, retire, or enter another profession.

Earnings

Beginning salaries vary greatly depending on where new public relations employees work. Some organizations tend to pay their employees far more than others. The highest-paying employers are manufacturers, utilities, and scientific and technical firms. Those paying the lowest salaries include museums and miscellaneous nonprofit organizations, religious and charitable organizations, and advertising agencies. The average salary for new graduates entering this field is more than $25,000 a year. While the median salary for all public relations specialists and managers is about $46,000 a year, some earn more than $100,000 a year.

An Interesting Career in Public Relations

Careers often start in unusual ways. Jeanne Krier was a housewife and mother working part-time in several libraries doing a story-hour show. It was quite a challenging job as she had to hold the

attention of fifty children and their mothers at each of four sessions every day. During this time, Jeanne spoke with a friend who
was writing a book about a baseball team and discovered that he
was having no luck in getting the team to support his efforts. He
had sent scores of letters to the team and never received a
response. Jeanne called the team for him but was unsuccessful in
gaining support. She then showed the local media sections of the
book, and they loved it. Then she went back to the team, and
everyone was now eager to provide the author with the team statistics and history.

Jeanne's career in public relations had been launched. She went
to work for the small trade publisher that was putting out the
baseball book and learned all the parts of publishing a book, from
editing to lifting boxes of books that needed to be stored. She also
demonstrated a tremendous facility for public relations. Although
the baseball book was a minor player in the vast publishing world,
Jeanne managed to get it reviewed on the "Today" show. Then she
organized a party in the ballpark on the day the book was published. Her efforts turned the book into a publishing success story.

From the small publisher, Jeanne went to a larger press, where
she had the job of publicizing the company's very academic titles.
Soon she decided that she wanted to go back to publicizing trade
books and also to work in New York City. She was able to get a job
in New York at a public relations firm that specialized in books.
Then after one year, Jeanne continued her rapid climb up the public relations ladder by becoming the public relations director of a
large educational publishing house. There she oversaw a department of ten people and did work in product, employee, event, and
financial public relations. After six years, Jeanne left this firm to
start her own company specializing in the niche of book publicity.
According to Jeanne, her job is fun because she believes in what
she is doing.

Jeanne has always been an extremely loquacious person and
thinks that both genes and destiny drew her to a public relations

career. As a child, she enjoyed standing in front of a group and performing, whether it was twirling a baton or tumbling. Later on, in high school and college, she learned communication skills through performing in the theater. Today, Jeanne uses her speaking and performance skills in her everyday work. About 50 percent of her daily activities involves talking. She spends a lot of time talking to the media in order to get the word out on the books she is publicizing. Jeanne also spends time talking to authors. Other tasks include managing events, writing speeches, and writing publicity blurbs for the press.

Career Advice. To be successful in public relations, Jeanne believes that you must do your homework and be persistent. She points out that when you want information, you must try every way to reach the people who have it. This public relations expert also feels that there is no substitute for learning how to use language well. To do that, you must know how language is structured.

Public Relations Agent

While Karen E. Polun's career in public relations demands a lot of talking, one of the most important elements of her success is the ability to speak persuasively. Although she is not a salesperson— she doesn't actually sell products—she is usually trying to persuade other parties to do something: to write a favorable story, to accept a creative strategy, or even to use her public relations agency over another. According to Karen, the more people you talk with, the more capable you are of talking with different types of people. She still remembers her first call to the media—she was a nervous wreck. Now, it's almost as if she's calling a friend. She has built a mental portfolio of what works and what doesn't in communicating with others.

Talking to the Press. Since people get so much of their information from the media, Karen spends considerable time every day communicating with different reporters across the country to ensure that they are writing or broadcasting information about her clients in as favorable a manner as possible.

Talking to Clients. One of Karen's clients, a major corporation, wants her firm to handle some general publicity events while another client, a major trade association, wants the firm to help improve the association's public image. She has to know how to communicate with each of her clients individually and effectively. She can't communicate with everyone in the same way. When talking to a client, Karen may be talking one-on-one, to a group of ten, or to a very large group.

Talking to Colleagues. Karen frequently has to talk with her colleagues. She may be involved in a creative brainstorming session with a group of coworkers or in a one-on-one strategy meeting with a partner.

Human Resources

Human resources staff members are the "people persons" in organizations. They try to find the best possible employees and match them to the jobs for which they are best suited. They are also involved in training, employee morale and productivity, corporate benefits programs, and labor relations. Because they work so closely with people, most human resources professionals must be able to communicate effectively. Recruiters, especially, need to be chatty types as they travel frequently to college campuses searching for promising job applicants. In the same way, headhunters (a nickname for those who search for executives to fill positions) must be extremely articulate.

Getting Started in Human Resources

For an entry-level job, you need to be a college graduate. While many schools have programs leading to a degree in human resources, employers often want people with a well-rounded liberal arts education. Should you decide to specialize in an area like labor relations, you might need to have an advanced degree in industrial or labor relations or even to be a lawyer. And, of course, knowledge of computers is important for most jobs.

Job Availability and Earnings

Jobs in human resources are not just at companies and organizations but at all types of employment agencies, from those seeking temporary workers to those looking for a new chief operating officer. The easiest place to get a job is with a rapidly expanding business; the hardest is with a firm or organization that is downsizing. Overall, the demand for people to work in human resources is growing.

If you majored in human resources in college, you could expect to start at nearly $37,000 a year. Human resource managers earn an average salary of $81,800 a year.

Businesses and Organizations Need Talkative Types

If you have the gift of gab and can communicate effectively, the careers in businesses and other organizations mentioned in this chapter will give you an opportunity to spend a great deal of time talking on the job. It is the receptionist who first presents the image of a company or organization to visitors. It is the marketer who determines the success of the sale of a product or a fundraising event, while the public relations professional builds positive images and relationships with the public. And, finally, it is the human resources officer who hires the people who run companies successfully.

CHAPTER FIVE

Ring! Ring!

Telephone Talkers

The telephone offers people a personal type of communication that cannot be obtained through the written word. Through billions of phone calls each day, Americans keep in touch with their families and friends, run businesses, obtain information and advice, purchase and sell goods and services, handle emergency situations, and communicate with each other in many other ways. Today, it is just about as easy to talk to someone in a remote part of the world as in your neighborhood, and you can make calls from your home, car, business, or wherever you happen to be.

Each year, the number of telephones in service dramatically increases, as do the many ways in which the phone is used. That means more jobs for those who wish to spend their working hours on the phone. Shortly after the invention of the telephone, most jobs that involved talking on the phone were as switchboard operators at telephone companies. Then jobs became available at businesses and large organizations that needed operators to route calls to the appropriate people.

Today, you can find a variety of jobs that keep you on the phone most of the day. You can sell products for telemarketers, take orders for catalog companies, conduct research for information companies and pollsters, handle complaints for businesses, provide information or special services for companies and organizations, field calls for politicians, work for a telephone answering service, offer help on a hotline, screen calls for a radio talk show, or take reservations for rock concerts or theater tickets. In each and every one of these jobs, you are able to use your gift of gab.

Telephone Operators

When the phone was first invented, telephone company operators had to direct each call to its destination. Customers would turn a crank on their phones to alert the operator, who would determine what number was desired by saying, "Number please," or, "Operator." The operator would then make the connection or indicate to the customer that the line was busy. Operators in the telephone exchanges in small towns and rural areas often carried on friendly conversations with callers. For example, they might indicate that the local doctor was not in his office but at the hospital, tell about recent births and deaths in the community, or chat briefly with customers they knew.

Technological inventions have largely changed the role of telephone company operators. Most telephone numbers are now dialed directly without the assistance of an operator, although operators do help place some calls. Today's telephone company central office operators help people with person-to-person or collect calls or with special billing requests, such as charging a call to a third number or giving customers credit or a refund for a wrong number or a bad connection. They are also called upon to handle emergency calls and assist children or people with physical limitations. Directory assistance operators answer inquiries for phone numbers by accessing computerized directories arranged alphabetically and geographically. Then the number is usually provided by a computerized recording.

Operators in Other Settings

Most telephone operators no longer work for phone companies. Instead, they are employed by hotels, hospitals, businesses, department stores, colleges, and other organizations where they run switchboards. It is their job to answer and relay outside calls, connect outgoing calls, connect interoffice calls, supply information to callers, and record messages. Many operators also act as receptionists (see Chapter 4), greeting and announcing visitors.

Operators on the Job

Being a telephone operator does not require much physical exertion, as you spend most of your day sitting in front of a switchboard handling calls. However, the pace can be hectic during peak calling periods when your board is lit up with calls. Although the work is quite repetitive, there is frequent opportunity to talk with people as you try to ascertain their needs. At a phone company, this could mean tracking down the George Johnson the customer wants. For example, is it the George Johnson who resides on Forest Drive or the one on Douglas Street? At businesses, hotels, and other organizations, you may have to chat with individuals to determine exactly who should handle their calls, or you may simply supply information, such as the address of your workplace or the hours it is open.

No matter where you work as a phone operator, you are more likely to be a full-time than a part-time employee. There is also the possibility of working shifts if your workplace operates around the clock as phone companies, hotels, and hospitals do. The hours you work are normally assigned by seniority, which lets the most experienced operators choose the hours they want to work.

What It Takes to Be a Phone Operator

Decidedly, you need to like talking on the phone for hours at a time. Another basic requirement for this job is having a clear, pleasing voice and good hearing. Since you will encounter people who are impatient, rude, and angry, the ability to be pleasant, courteous, and patient under trying circumstances is essential. In addition to being a good talker, you need to be an effective listener. And good eye-hand coordination and manual dexterity are useful. This is one job where you may not need to have a high school diploma, although many employers require one. For some jobs as an operator, fluency in a foreign language is a definite asset.

Training

Whether you work at a phone company or some other organization, you will be trained to use the equipment. At phone companies, you can expect to have classroom instruction, which lasts up to three weeks and is followed by on-the-job training. Classroom instruction even covers geography, so that you know where major cities are. Tapes are used to familiarize you with the dial tone, busy signal, and other telephone sounds. You also use tapes to study recordings of your own voice so you can improve your speaking voice and phone courtesy. Training at businesses, hospitals, and other organizations is usually shorter and less formal. Typically, you learn your job from experienced workers.

Answering the Phone at a Publishing House

Although he works as a customer service representative and order taker at a book publishing house, Don Moorhead also fills in as a switchboard operator when one of the two full-time operators goes on vacation or is sick. As an operator, he wears headphones and sits in front of a large phone console that has a regular dialing pad. Seven phone lines feed into the console, but even more calls may be awaiting his attention in the phone queue. At busy times, there may be as many as ten calls waiting to be answered. Curiously, automation has made Don's work more personal. Individuals who know the extension numbers of company employees dial them directly, while those who speak to Don usually need information directing them to the correct employee to handle their concerns. Most calls are short, usually fifteen seconds or less, but they do require Don to keep current with who is handling different aspects of business at the publishing house. He keeps notes that tell him who has changed job responsibilities. Don finds this job interesting because he is serving as the front person for the company, and his conversation is often the first contact an individual has with his company.

Earnings

The earnings of a telephone operator average about $540 a week for those who are employed at telephone companies. For those who work at a switchboard at a business, hotel, hospital, or other organization, the average weekly earnings are about $415. Telephone operators who work for phone companies have higher hourly earnings because they are members of unions. These union contracts also provide for extra pay for work beyond the normal work hours as well as for Sunday, holiday, and night-shift work. They also spell out the time required to advance from the lowest-paying, nonsupervisory operator position to the highest. It usually takes four years.

The Future Job Picture

Technology is reducing the number of jobs for telephone operators as automation eliminates jobs and increases each operator's productivity. It is especially affecting the number of jobs for operators in telephone companies. Many telephone companies do not plan to replace operators who leave and are laying off other operators. In the business world, older switchboards that require operators to make connections are being replaced by ones that route calls automatically. Furthermore, voice message systems have reduced the need for operators. Nevertheless, many firms and other organizations still want to have operators for the personal touch that technology cannot offer.

Telemarketers

When you think of a job in telemarketing, you may think it's just a job making phone calls trying to sell anything from magazines to carpet cleaning. Much more is involved in telemarketing, however, which a majority of businesses now use in some form. While outbound telemarketing calls often deal with direct sales, as you might expect, they also involve soliciting for charities, doing market research, making appointments, providing information, and auditing customer service and product satisfaction. Telemarketers also handle an immense volume of inbound calls, from processing orders and making reservations to registering products, providing information, and serving as message takers. If you choose to work in telemarketing, you may find a job as one of thousands of professionally trained service agents for a huge telemarketing firm handling both inbound and outbound calls or as one of a handful of employees at a small telemarketing firm that specializes in a particular type of call.

Coastal Communications

Coastal Communications is a small telemarketing and order-taking service that employs twenty individuals. While the firm primarily handles incoming calls from individuals wishing to reach their doctors, it also serves as a voice-mail center for clients, takes orders for businesses, and makes some outbound sales calls. The company is now twenty years old and was purchased five years ago by Sara Henderson. At the time, Sara was a recent college graduate with a degree in marketing. Since then, she has become a computer expert in order to set up systems capable of handling the fifty-five hundred calls the firm answers each day. According to Sara, firms like hers must modernize or go out of business.

Prerequisites for Employment. Sara looks for phone operators who speak fluent, understandable English and can type. Prospective employees must pass spelling, grammar, writing, and number tests because she needs employees who can spell names correctly, get phone numbers down without transposing numbers, and write easily understandable messages for her customers. Sara also wants to hire self-confident individuals who are not intimidated by angry phone callers who may yell at them.

Training for the Job. One of the first things that Sara's new employees must learn how to do is to speak with a smile in their voices, especially as they handle common phrases used in most calls. Then her customers know at once that the phone operator is there to help them. Training of new operators is on-the-job and usually takes from ten days to three weeks working with a supervisor. New employees have to learn a special computer keyboard with fifty buttons used to handle different functions such as saving messages, patching calls to other numbers, and delivering messages. At first, the trainer talks on the phone as the new employee types so the employee learns about the calls and accounts. Then the trainee types and handles simple calls under the trainer's supervision for a week before handling calls alone. It takes approximately six weeks for new employees to become speedy operators capable of handling all calls.

On the Job. A lot of talking is involved in this job, which makes it a perfect choice for talkative types. An average operator handles from five hundred to seven hundred calls in an eight-hour shift. During rush hours, two to three callers are often on hold, so calls must be handled very quickly. The operators wear headsets and sit in front of computers. A glance at the screen tells them what type of call they are answering and provides information on one side of the screen on how the call should be answered. The other side of the screen has space for typing information to be sent to the firm's customers. Operators must talk and type at the same time. A good operator should be able to get a lot of information from what the caller says and not have to ask too many questions.

Jobs at Sara's company are interesting for operators because there is so much variety in the type of calls. The operators never know whom they will be talking to next. All of her employees are hourly workers who receive benefits after three months if they work full-time.

Zacson Corporation

Even though Zacson Corporation has eight hundred seats for telephone sales representatives, the company is only considered a medium-size telemarketing firm as there are companies that have as many as two thousand seats. Zacson Corporation is seventeen years old and now has nine telemarketing locations in the United States and three centers in foreign countries. The company makes and receives calls for telecommunications, finance, high technology, and utility companies. Its employees usually find out about positions at the company through newspaper ads and employee referrals.

Training Program. It takes both time and effort to become a telephone sales representative for Zacson. New employees must spend one to two weeks in the classroom. After one day of orientation, approximately 20 percent of the remaining time is devoted to learning the equipment and sales techniques, while 80 percent is spent on learning all about the product that the trainee will be selling. The knowledge that has to be absorbed about a product may consist of two hundred to three hundred pages of information. Once training is completed, the new representative is seated next to a representative with three to four years of sales experience who will be able to provide any necessary help. Originally, employees are trained only on one product; however, as they become more experienced, they may learn to handle two or three more products.

On the Job. Telephone sales representatives sit in their own cubicles in front of a computer. On the walls, they typically tack up pertinent information about a product so they won't have to use the product book during most phone calls. Depending on the complexity of the product that they are selling, representatives may dial 250 to 350 calls a day. While they are talking, they also have to be typing information. This is not an easy task. Being a sales representative is a demanding job in which one call after another must be handled. Experienced representatives may alternate between making calls and taking calls and can be handling as many as four products. This requires concentration!

The Future Is Golden

This is the gold-rush time of telemarketing as more and more companies are beginning to use telemarketing firms to sell their products or services, do research on customer satisfaction, or act as their customer service representatives. It is estimated that in the next few years the demand for new telephone sales representatives will be extremely high. Since so many new people are entering this field, opportunities for a rapid advance up the telemarketing career path are excellent. Furthermore, there is opportunity to work in this field full-time or part-time.

Hotlines and Help Lines

Hotlines and help lines are designed to provide special assistance to people who have a wide range of needs. There are lines that put runaway teens in contact with their parents, lines that provide help with income taxes, lines that provide help to victims of many diseases, and many more, as you can see from the following list of help line subjects:

- adoption and foster care
- AIDS
- alcohol and drug abuse
- child abuse and family violence
- child care

- consumer information
- counseling
- crisis intervention
- death and dying
- disability services
- disaster services
- driver information
- education
- employment
- environmental resources
- family planning
- financial assistance
- health care
- housing
- immigration
- legal services
- mental health
- missing children and runaways
- mother and infant health
- poison control
- rape and sexual assault
- recycling
- refugee services
- senior services
- suicide prevention
- tax services
- veteran services
- youth and teen services

While calls on these lines may be answered by volunteers, many are answered by paid employees. Some hotlines and help lines concentrate on providing information, while others offer counseling to individuals who have serious problems. On many of these lines, an ability to listen to the caller plays as important a role as the ability to communicate effectively. Talkers who are articulate may really enjoy working on hotlines and help lines because what they say is not usually scripted. Instead, they are responding to the individual caller's needs.

There are no educational requirements to handle calls on many of these lines, nor is a particular background desired. However, some lines do require a specific expertise, such as for handling calls on taxes or poison control. On lines where the operator serves as a counselor, it is important for the operator to be non-judgmental and skilled in helping callers understand the consequences of their choices. Quite often, counselors need to reflect back what they hear so that callers can gain a better understanding of possible solutions to their problems. Before anyone starts to work on a hotline, there is always an intensive training program that includes segments on procedures, listening, talking, and subject information.

A Closer Look at Hotline and Help Line Jobs

When you work on a hotline or help line, you are usually an hourly worker and can work either full-time or part-time. Entry-level workers may begin with hourly wages as high as $10 per hour and can earn up to $15 with experience. If you work full-time, you can expect to receive some benefits after three to six months of employment. On many lines, you work shifts because calls are received twenty-four hours a day, seven days a week. The hours that employees work are largely determined by the times the lines receive the highest volume of calls. The length of time that you devote to a call depends on the nature of the call. Information calls may be as brief as four to five minutes, while referral calls can last from five to ten minutes. The longest calls involve actual counseling and may run from twenty-five to thirty minutes or longer.

While being able to provide help to people offers immense satisfaction, at the same time you can experience the frustration of not knowing the outcome of the work that you do each day. The burnout rate is quite high for people working on emotionally draining hotlines covering topics such as child abuse, suicide prevention, and drug abuse. Few people stay in these jobs for more than a few years. Some hotline and help line employees advance to become trainers and supervisors of other employees and handle only the most challenging calls.

Working on a Library Information Line

The phone calls come in one right after another for Karen Madigan, who spends part of her time as a librarian in a county library giving callers the answers to questions about topics ranging from the gross national product of Mexico in 1997 to John Wayne's real name. Her workplace is a desk in the reference section not far from where books are checked out. While she and another librarian are giving information to callers, two other reference librarians are busily helping patrons in the library with their research needs. At this library, there are nine other librarians who take shifts answering the phones. On a typical one-hour shift, Karen talks to as many as ten to twelve callers. She especially likes the fact that she comes into contact with such a wide variety of people on this job. To find the answers to a caller's questions, she has a computer in front of her and is surrounded by reference books. She uses the computer to find information in about 80 percent of the cases.

Karen has a master's degree in library science, and she is continually taking courses and workshops in subjects such as database searching and the Internet to keep up with changes in the field. She gained the verbal skills she uses on the job by learning a technique called the "reference interview" in library school. This is a method of learning exactly what people who ask librarians questions really want to know, which, according to Karen, isn't always what they ask at first.

To young people who would like to have a job like hers, Karen advises that listening to people and really hearing what they say is more important than talking to them. She believes that you can be very effective in the job if you are really interested in callers and enjoy putting them at ease.

Although Karen only spends part of her shift answering calls, there are librarians who spend the entire workday on the phone researching questions for callers. To handle this job, you need to be a trained librarian or have solid research skills.

Customer Service Representatives

As a customer service representative (CSR), you never stop talking to your company's customers while on the job. What you talk about, however, varies with the company where you work. You may find yourself taking orders, troubleshooting problems, or providing some type of special service. Because many companies keep their customer service lines open longer than the typical workday, you may find yourself beginning work quite early or working until late in the evening. Because business is currently booming, there is a considerable demand for customer service representatives.

Earnings

Customer service representatives earn an average of $27,000 per year. CSRs who work evenings, nights, weekends, or holidays are often paid a shift differential in addition to the hourly rate.

Working as a CSR for a Major Newspaper Group

The responsibilities of a customer service representative at this newspaper group in Northern California include handling vacation hold requests, billing questions, and delivery problems, as well as providing general information about two newspapers. There are more than fifty full-time and part-time customer service representatives who handle the daily calls. Sunday morning is the busiest time, when there may be as many as 120 calls on hold. It is not easy to pass the rigorous three-week training program to become a CSR for the newspapers. There are daylong tests on which you must score 90 percent or better, plus a two-day final. In a class of six to eight trainees, only two usually graduate. Graduates are on call at first before they are assigned a regular shift. All the representatives are members of a union and are hourly employees. Being a CSR is just the first step on a career ladder that can lead to a management position. Representatives can become part of the VIP desk, which handles difficult customers and questions and makes callbacks to customers. There is also the opportunity to become a trainer, as new CSR classes are being held almost continuously, or to move on to a position as a supervisor.

Working as a CSR for a Book Publisher

Earlier in this chapter, you met Don Moorhead, who fills in occasionally as a phone operator at the book publishing company where he works. His major job, however, is as a customer service representative with two responsibilities: handling calls from customers who have problems or want information and taking orders for books. Don is a college graduate with a major in sociology, although most of his twenty-five coworkers were English majors. Some of them see this job as a stepping-stone into the publishing world, while Don wants to use the experience he has gained talking to customers to become a radio personality. When he was hired as a CSR, the company was looking for people who had a good phone presence and could understand what callers wanted. Don fit these requirements because he had always been a talker and had some radio and improvisation comedy experience. He does use his great sense of humor when it is appropriate to do so in handling calls.

All of the customer service representatives at the publishing house are hourly employees and have benefits packages. They work varying shifts, which may begin as early as 7:00 A.M. or end at 7:00 P.M. Each representative now works from a small cubicle, which Don likes because you don't hear the other representatives speaking. Formerly, all of the representatives were in a large, open room, which made for a noisy work area. Don and the other customer service representatives learn their skills on the job from supervisors, managers, and coworkers. There is no formal training program. Some opportunity for advancement exists for representatives to become supervisors and then managers.

The stream of calls to Don and the other customer service representatives is steady. When they are not really busy, the representatives do paperwork on orders. The calls come from an automated menu, and customers stay on hold until a representative is available. When Don gets a call requesting information, he uses his computer to answer questions about book titles, prices, and availability. He also has to resolve problems such as damaged books, incorrect shipments, and mispriced items. Don initiates the solution for each problem and puts it into his computer. For example, he could order another book to be sent to a customer who received a damaged book. When Don takes calls to order books, he must follow these steps:

1. Determine the name of the customer and if he or she has an account with the company.
2. Access the account on the computer, if there is one.
3. Find out what the customer needs.
4. Agree on the payment method.

While Don is talking to the customer, he is entering the order as they talk. Overnight, the orders are printed to an invoice and sent to the warehouse.

Don likes his job as a customer service representative because he enjoys the contact with different people and not having to read from a script. He regrets that he only talks to people once and doesn't get to know them in this job. Don is also sorry that some people take their anger out on him and won't give him a chance to resolve a problem.

Working as a CSR for a Catalog Company

Maggie Seibel handles orders and customer complaints for a company that sells a wide range of products in its catalog. On the job, she talks all the time. There is scarcely ever more than a few moments between calls. As she answers each call, the company expects her to establish a friendly relationship quickly with the caller. She may help a woman select the right musical instrument for her child, answer a question about the size or color of a blouse, or process an order for a pair of shoes. Maggie has to be very knowledgeable about the products in the catalog to handle this job. She received training for one month, eight hours a day, before she ever answered any phone calls, and then she was assigned to work with someone for one week. Her calls are randomly monitored even now.

Maggie is between careers right now, working as a CSR while completing her doctorate in psychology. She is a college graduate with both bachelor's and master's degrees. She finds that many of the other phone representatives have college degrees.

For Maggie, vocabulary is fun and has led to her facility with words. She has always done crossword puzzles, loves vocabulary games, and picks up a dictionary every day to learn a new word. This talkative person first knew in elementary school that she wanted to have a job that would require a lot of talking. Her teacher would let Maggie use a pretend microphone to conduct interviews with other children who would act as historical figures. Maggie would interview the person with questions like, "So, Betsy Ross, how did you get the idea for the flag?" Today, Maggie brings all her past verbal experiences—which include stints as a teacher, psychologist, and retail store owner—into her present job.

Technical Support Representatives

As technology brings new products to the market at a dizzying pace, a need has arisen for people who can tell us how to handle problems with such products as copiers, video cameras, telephone answering machines, DVD players, and especially computers and computer software. These troubleshooters who help us when we can't make multiple copies of a document, program the TiVo to record a specific program, or send an e-mail message are known as technical support representatives. All receive considerable on-the-job training to learn about typical problems and how to help people work through them step by step. Many, especially those working in the computer industry, must have considerable expertise to be hired as support representatives. This is a career where scientific and engineering expertise can be coupled with a desire to talk with people. In this job, representatives may spend considerable time on the phone helping individual callers.

Dispatchers

The work of dispatchers varies greatly; however, all dispatchers have one thing in common—they spend their days on the phone. Police, fire, and ambulance dispatchers, also called public-safety dispatchers, handle calls from people reporting crimes, fires, and medical emergencies. Taxicab dispatchers relay requests for cabs to individual drivers; tow-truck dispatchers take calls for emergency road service; and utility-company dispatchers handle calls related to electiricty, gas, and phone service.

On the job, dispatchers sit for long periods of time in typical office surroundings. Their work can become very hectic when large numbers of calls come in at the same time. Being a public-safety dispatcher is especially stressful because slow or improper responses can result in further destruction of property, serious injury, or even death. No matter where they work, all dispatchers have to keep records of all the calls they receive and the actions they take.

Police, ambulance, taxicab, and tow-truck dispatchers often work as part of a two-person team in large communication centers or companies. One dispatcher usually receives incoming calls while the other dispatches help and follows up on the calls.

Training

Most dispatchers develop the necessary skills on the job. Working under an experienced dispatcher, they monitor calls and learn how to operate telephones, radio transmitters and receivers, radio consoles, teletypewriters, and data communications terminals. Once they gain confidence, they begin to handle calls themselves. Many police, fire, and ambulance dispatchers enroll in a course designed by the Associated Public Safety Communications Officers (APSCO), which covers topics such as overview of the police, fire, and rescue functions; modern public safety telecommunications systems; and national crime information computer systems. Emergency medical dispatchers often get special training or have special skills. Some states require public-safety dispatchers to have a certificate to work on a state network. Voluntary certification is available through APSCO and the International Municipal Signal Association.

Earnings and Job Opportunities

The average yearly earnings of public-safety dispatchers are $29,000. There is considerable turnover in these positions, which increases the opportunity for jobs. Overall, the occupation is expected to grow due to population growth.

A Police Dispatcher

For sixteen years, Joanne Earle has taken 9-1-1 calls and other emergency calls in a suburban county for ten police agencies and the sheriff's office. This is a job where she never stops talking. Joanne sits in front of a computer wearing headphones, as do the six to nine other dispatchers on her shift. When a call comes in, she enters pertinent data in the computer. Another dispatcher sees the information on his or her screen and takes the appropriate steps to dispatch help, if needed. The dispatchers rotate their jobs around the room. If a call comes in concerning a fire or medical emergency, it is immediately transferred to the fire department.

Joanne would never consider having another career. Although being a dispatcher means seeing much of the seamy side of life, including people hurting each other, it is a genuine opportunity to help people. Also, she appreciates the outstanding teamwork with her fellow dispatchers. In addition, she thrives on the adrenaline and knows that she would find any other job boring. In this job, every call is different. She can never predict what it will be, especially since she usually works the 3:00 P.M. to 11:00 P.M. shift, which is the busiest time with the most crime. Often, she has to keep callers on the phone when they are observing a crime so they can keep her updated about what is happening until an officer arrives on the scene. For Joanne, one of the few negatives to this career is having to work holidays and overtime.

Training. After Joanne was hired as a police dispatcher, she spent two and a half months in a classroom at a training center learning how to handle calls. She had to learn the police codes; for example, if a police officer pulls a car over, it is a code 1195. Joanne also learned policy and procedure and had to study both the penal code and the vehicle code. Plus, she spent time learning how to operate the computer-aided dispatch system. Before Joanne began to take calls, she worked one-on-one with a seasoned dispatcher.

A Look Ahead

If you are a talkative type, jobs involving the use of the phone throughout the workday are a perfect career choice. The only negative on the horizon is the fact that more phone jobs will be handled by automated systems in the future. The rosiest side of the employment picture is for those who are interested in telemarketing careers.

CHAPTER SIX

Talking Professions

Teachers, Doctors, Lawyers, Politicians, and Clerics

U sing your gift of gab to instruct the young, heal the sick, comfort the hurting, or protect the rights of others is truly rewarding. Teachers, doctors, lawyers, politicians, and clerics have chosen professions in which they do a lot of talking. Think of the college professor standing before classes and lecturing for an hour or more, or the doctor asking questions to arrive at a diagnosis. Then there is the trial lawyer who must speak effectively to plead a case before a jury. On the campaign stump or spearheading a filibuster, being a senator is a nonstop talking career. And members of the clergy of all faiths talk regularly to members of their congregations in formal and informal situations. Should you decide on one of these well-known careers, you will have to acquire a specialized knowledge, usually through extensive academic preparation.

Teachers

Scholars like Aristotle, Plato, and Socrates were all great talkers and renowned teachers. The first ordinary citizen to be selected by NASA to participate in a space-shuttle mission was a teacher. Former President Lyndon Baines Johnson's first job was as a teacher. Ask people to name someone who had a profound influence on their lives, and many will answer with the name of a teacher.

When you think of a job as a teacher, you may think only of a career in a kindergarten, elementary, secondary, or college classroom. Broader options exist. You could teach someone to make welds, clean teeth, or fix a computer in a vocational school, or you could teach someone to read or play chess in an adult education class. Nevertheless, wherever you elect to teach, this is one job in which what you say can decidedly influence the lives of others.

Preparation for a Teaching Job

Today, anyone planning to teach, whether in a kindergarten or at the college level, needs at least a bachelor's degree. Many elementary and secondary teachers also need master's degrees, and it is almost essential to have a doctorate in order to teach at the college level. Before you can teach in a public school classroom from kindergarten through high school, you need to meet your state's requirements for teacher certification. These requirements deal with the college courses that teachers must complete satisfactorily to become certified. You do not need a license to teach in a college or university; however, in some states you need one for jobs in private schools and community colleges.

Teachers' Salaries

Teachers' salaries are constantly increasing, although they do vary greatly between states. If you start teaching in an elementary or secondary school today your salary will probably be between $26,700 and $31,100. Then you can expect annual increases based on your years of experience and educational degrees and, in some school districts, on merit. The average salary for full-time college faculty on nine-month contracts averages about $68,000 a year. You will earn even more money if you teach in a field such as medicine, law, engineering, or business.

Changes in Teaching

As a teacher at any level, from preschool through college, you will use your verbal skills to introduce your students to subject matter, whether it is the ABCs or the theory of relativity. The role of the teacher is changing from that of lecturer or presenter to one of facilitator or coach. Interactive discussion and hands-on learning are replacing rote memorization. You will be challenged daily to provide interesting, exciting, and motivating ideas that make your students, regardless of their ages, want to learn. You'll use games, music, art, and props to help younger children learn and help older students delve more deeply into subjects. At all levels, you will need to make the computer a part of your curriculum. Besides using your verbal skills to teach, you will be called on to use them regularly to speak to your colleagues and the parents of your students.

Teaching at the Elementary Level

In the past ten years, Andy Poon has taught elementary school classes from first through fourth grade. Right now, he is teaching a rather unusual first-grade class in which three-fourths of the children speak English as their second language. In this class, when Andy speaks, he often acts out what he is saying. For example, as Andy tells the children how to use the pencil sharpener, he is also showing them how at the same time. The nature of this class makes it essential for him to talk more than the typical first-grade teacher might talk. Of course, Andy also does the same routine talking that most teachers do—greeting children in the morning, giving directions, going over work, explaining new concepts, keeping the children on task, and bidding them good-bye at the end of the day. Andy admits to being a chatty person who likes to talk a lot and feels that teaching is a perfect job for his talkative nature.

Teaching at the Junior High Level

Not only does Meg Sutherland spend a great deal of time in the classroom speaking to the students in her four language-arts classes, she spends hours outside the classroom planning what she is going to say to them. This is one aspect of teaching that many prospective teachers may not have considered. Teachers must be well prepared before speaking in the classroom.

Meg's school is a site-managed school, which means all the teachers are on teams that make many of the decisions on how the children will be educated. Meg works on a team with parents, coworkers, administrators, and community members. Meg believes that she gained her facility with words through being involved in high school organizations in which she had to give speeches in front of groups.

Teaching at the Junior and Senior High Levels

Joanna Oberthur is a junior and senior high school math teacher who spends her days explaining mathematical concepts to her students. This is a challenging task because she must think of several different ways to say the same thing in order to reach all of her students. Teachers can never be complacent and think that one explanation will be suitable for all their students. Joanna firmly believes that if everyone in the classroom does not understand what she is saying, she has not done her job successfully. Besides teaching math, Joanna is the coach of the girls' volleyball and basketball teams, which also requires her to talk a lot as students prepare for and play games. Joanna uses what she learned in earning bachelor's degrees in recreation and mathematics as well as her master's degree in education to handle her present job, which consists of eight hours of teaching math and one and one-half hours of coaching every day. Joanna's job is so talk-intensive that she spends 80 percent of her time at work talking.

Teaching at the College Level

In many college courses, the professors spend the entire class period lecturing. Students on college campuses quickly learn who the excellent lecturers are—the ones who make the material come alive for them. In this job, it is not sufficient to speak well; it is also absolutely essential to have an excellent grasp of the material—based on years of previous and continuing research. Of course, talking is not limited to the classroom—professors hold office hours to advise and guide students in their work and often present their research papers at professional conferences.

Teaching Adult Education

Many adults have not completed their education and need remedial work to improve their basic skills or earn a high school equivalency diploma. Others want to learn skills for jobs that do not require a college degree, such as welder, dental hygienist, x-ray technician, or cosmetologist. Some adults simply want to acquire a new skill, from quilting to using new software programs. They may take a class such as cooking, dancing, or photography for personal enrichment. About half of all the teachers working with adults are part-time teachers. Training requirements vary from needing a degree to just being an expert in something like flower arranging or physical fitness. Just like all other teachers, adult education teachers need to be capable speakers.

Adult Education at a General Motors Plant

Carolyn L. Kramer teaches adult employees and their spouses at a General Motors plant. In addition to teaching, Carolyn must first recruit students. The recruitment process involves going into the factories and speaking to employees, speaking at meetings, conferring with educational counselors, and answering questions. Carolyn then schedules sessions that require her to converse, usually over the phone, with the new student about his or her educational goals. Many of the students often need advice on other matters, too. Carolyn also gives workshops for other teachers. Besides having held a variety of jobs—including waitress, tutor, and copy clerk—that helped her prepare for the talking side of her career, she also has a bachelor's degree in business education and is working on a master's degree in adult education.

An Instructor in Adult Basic Education

Sara Gutting teaches adults reading, writing, and mathematics up to the eighth-grade level and prepares adults to take the General Educational Development (GED) examination, which, if they pass, gives them the equivalent of a high school diploma. Sara even teaches some of her GED classes at a local jail. She works with small groups, individuals, and some large groups. She also performs workshops for adult counselors and learners.

Sara started on this career path working as an intern/student teacher in a high school dropout program for youth. She ended up getting her first job there teaching preemployment skills and then the GED. In this setting, working with groups of twelve to eighteen students, Sara learned how to talk and listen to students. Her educational background includes a bachelor's degree in secondary education with concentrations in English, speech communications, and theater. For Sara, the only negative to her career is that most of her teaching is done at night. This is a common complaint of adult education teachers, who must accommodate the job and family responsibilities of their students by teaching classes at nights and on weekends.

An Education Administrator

The career path for many teachers leads to becoming administrators—deans, principals, curriculum directors, assistant superintendents, and superintendents. Carolyn Hagerty Heier was the director of education for the Department of Corrections, which is the same as being superintendent of a school corporation. For administrators, she believes there are four steps in the communication process:

1. Plan, in groups, every aspect of a program.
2. Organize, which involves determining how the plan will be accomplished. In this step, an administrator delegates assignments to others so that the goals are accomplished in a timely fashion.

3. Move into action so all the tasks are accomplished.
4. Supervise the program, which involves working with people day to day.

Carolyn likes the talking aspects of administration but stresses that you must know the audience to whom you are speaking and adjust your vocabulary appropriately because not everyone is an expert on the jargon of this profession. Administrators speak about their programs to parents, the public, students, and peers. They also communicate with advisory committees, their own supervisors, and clerical staff. For this position, Carolyn needed to obtain a superintendent's license as well as be an effective communicator.

Doctors

In order to treat people effectively, doctors need to be good communicators. What doctors say can have a very substantial effect on their patients' lives. Besides using their diagnostic skills, they must use their verbal skills to determine what is wrong with a patient. For example, if a patient is complaining of headaches, a doctor needs to know about their severity, frequency, and exact location. Doctors also need to be skilled speakers when they counsel patients on diet, preventive health care, and treatment regimens. Patients definitely have to understand whether they should soak an injured ankle in hot, warm, or ice water. And, of course, they must know how much medication to take and when to take it.

Unlike their predecessors, today's newly trained physicians face radically different choices of where and how to practice. Many are less likely to enter solo practice and more likely to take salaried jobs in group medical practices, clinics, and HMOs in order to have regular work hours and the opportunity for peer consultation. Others take salaried positions simply because they cannot afford the high cost of establishing a private practice while paying off student loans.

If you become a doctor, expect to work long, irregular hours— as many as sixty hours a week or more. The pace only lightens as you approach retirement and accept fewer new patients. Furthermore, the path to becoming a doctor is quite arduous, typically requiring thirteen years: four years of college, four years of medical school, a year as an intern, and three to eight years of residency, depending on the specialty. Once you become a doctor, the outlook for employment is excellent due to continued expansion of the health industry.

New technologies permit increasingly intensive care. Physicians can do additional tests, perform more procedures, and treat conditions previously regarded as untreatable. In addition, the population is growing and aging, and health care needs increase sharply with age.

Earnings

Doctors have among the highest earnings of any career. The average net income of doctors after expenses is more than $193,000 per year. Doctors who specialize in an area of medicine can earn significantly more than doctors in general practice.

A Pediatrician's Advice About Medical School

Caring for children is as rewarding as ever for Dr. Gustave (Stavie) Kreh, a pediatrician who adores children. He wants students who are thinking about becoming doctors to realize that medical school is a tough grind even for students who did well in high school and college. Most medical students are overwhelmed by the tremendous amount of study and memorization that is required their freshman year. Stavie still remembers the first day of medical school, when he could not even pronounce the words on the professors' mimeographed handouts. Challenged by the difficulty and amount of work that was required of him, he battled back by studying eight to ten hours a day in class and then four or five more hours in the library at night.

A Medical Specialist

Timothy A. Goedde, M.D., is a surgical oncologist whose specialty is the diagnosis and treatment of breast problems. This includes many benign diseases but also breast cancer. Breast disease in general—and breast cancer specifically—is a very emotional disease. It is extremely important for Timothy to keep his patients informed every step of the way in their treatment. This requires talking to them about their options as well as his recommendations. At times, his consultations take one to two hours, especially if the patient has been diagnosed with breast cancer, as the treatment can be complex and a host of factors go into the decision-making process. Timothy has found that patients do much better if they understand all the factors involved.

During his fellowship in surgical oncology at Roswell Park Cancer Institute, where he treated people with many different types of cancer, Timothy discovered that he wanted a job that involved a lot of talking. It became apparent to him that women with breast cancer needed the most help in terms of the information they receive and how they assimilate it and that most of them were either getting poor advice or were not able to understand all of the implications of the decisions they were being asked to make. Today, he finds it gratifying to use his verbal skills to make a bad situation less traumatic for someone who is very scared when she comes into his office.

....

Lawyers

Most people understand that lawyers, also called attorneys, are talkers from watching them in film and television dramas, and this is largely true in real life. As advocates, they represent one of the opposing parties in criminal and civil trials by presenting evidence that supports their clients or the government in court. This requires considerable talking in the courtroom as they participate in the selection of a jury, make opening statements, question witnesses, and sum everything up in a closing statement. As advisors, lawyers counsel their clients as to their legal rights and obligations and suggest particular courses of action in business and personal matters. Whether acting as advocates or advisors, all lawyers interpret the law and apply it to specific situations. Lawyers need to have excellent communication skills and deal with people in a courteous, efficient manner. They must never disclose matters discussed in confidence with their clients.

In order to practice law in the courts, you must be licensed or admitted to the bar in the state in which you wish to practice. For admission to the bar, you must pass a written examination. To qualify for this test, you usually have to have completed at least three years of college and graduated from an approved law school.

On the job, you are most likely to work for a small firm with fewer than five lawyers. Most of your work is done in your office, law libraries, and courtrooms. When a case is being tried, you can expect to work long hours.

Earnings

Lawyers' salaries increase as their responsibilities increase. As a beginning lawyer, you could expect to earn about $55,000, unless you obtained a job at one of the nation's largest law firms, where you might start at more than $80,000 a year. The average salary for all lawyers is about $95,000 per year.

A Lawyer in Private Practice

David F. Tudor is a lawyer working in a small firm with two paralegals. His days are spent talking to clients on the telephone or in his office about their legal problems and speaking for them in court. Although David's days vary, he usually talks two-thirds of a day and listens during the other third. He practices in three primary areas of law: criminal, family, and governmental law. While he typically deals with the same public officials, his clients are constantly changing. In preparing to handle a case, he first talks at length with his client and may talk to another lawyer or his office staff about preparing documents to file with the court. Then David may talk to other people involved in the case or to their lawyers. At a pretrial hearing, he may talk to the judge and other lawyers. Throughout a case, he is talking constantly with his client.

Career Advice. David feels that it is very important for prospective lawyers to learn to speak clearly and in a manner that people understand so a jury understands what they are talking about.

Politicians

President John F. Kennedy, Senator Richard Lugar, Congressman Sam Rayburn, and thousands of others who are or were involved in the running of the government are all politicians. Of course, your name does not have to be known around the country for you to be a politician. There are many positions at the state and local level—from state attorney general to mayor to city council representative.

Politics is a profession in which a way with words is absolutely essential. You must be able to talk in such a way that people will want to cast their votes for you. And in today's media-dominated culture, this means being able to talk effectively on television. Once you are elected, it is essential to use your verbal skills to get other politicians to agree with your viewpoint in order to enact laws or successfully govern a nation, state, or city. At the same time, politicians must continue to talk to the public to inform them of what they are doing or hope to do in office.

Earnings and Career Path

The salaries of politicians are set by laws. Excluding the president and vice president, the politicians who earn the largest salaries are those in the biggest cities and states. Typically, politicians begin on the local level, move to positions in state politics, and then to the national arena. Many politicians began their careers in high school running for different offices. Also, a great number of politicians are lawyers.

A Politician Who Became President

Lyndon B. Johnson entered politics when he was only twenty-three years old. After graduation from college, Johnson became a schoolteacher. Within a couple of years, he was writing speeches for a Democrat running for the House of Representatives. When this man was elected, Johnson went with him to Washington as his secretary. It has been said that within a few months he knew how to operate in Washington better than some who had been there twenty years before him. Four years later, he was appointed a Texas state administrator of the National Youth Administration by President Franklin Roosevelt. Then, just six years after entering politics, he ran for and was elected to Congress from the Tenth Congressional District of Texas. His meteoric climb in politics continued as he was elected to the United States Senate in 1948, where he served as both minority and majority leader. In 1960, he campaigned for the presidency; however, the Democrats chose John F. Kennedy as their candidate and Johnson was chosen to run as vice president. He became president in 1963 after the assassination of Kennedy and was elected president in 1964. Johnson loved to talk. Throughout his presidency, he often spoke at several occasions in a day. He even talked with tourists visiting the White House.

....

Clerics

Religious beliefs play a significant role in the lives of millions of Americans and prompt them to participate in organizations that reinforce their faith. Clerics, or members of the clergy, are the religious and spiritual leaders, the teachers and interpreters, of their traditions and faith. They organize and lead regular religious services on the Sabbath and on religious holidays, and they conduct special wedding and funeral ceremonies upon request. They may lead worshippers in prayers, administer sacraments, deliver sermons, and read from sacred texts such as the Bible, Talmud, or Koran.

Clerics are frequently called upon to visit the sick, comfort the dying and their families, and provide counseling to those in need. Their involvement in so many activities may cause members of the clergy to work from early in the morning until late at night, seven days a week. Their training usually consists of a course of study at a seminary.

A Roman Catholic Priest

Father Tom Clegg does considerable talking as pastor of the Good Shepherd parish. He did not set out to find a career in which he could talk a lot but rather was looking for a job in which he could serve people. Father Tom particularly enjoys conversing with his congregation about religion and faith. He also spends considerable time talking when he is counseling or giving spiritual direction. And he spends time in meetings associated with the church as well as in teaching and interacting with people of all age levels, from adults to children.

Father Tom believes that he acquired many of his verbal skills by being part of a family with ten children. In his family, you had to be an effective speaker to get what you wanted. He further honed his talking skills by being involved in many organizations.

A Rabbi of a Congregation in a Large City

Rabbi Jonathan Stein of the Reform branch of Judaism was attracted to the rabbinate because it allowed him to use his skills and talents in a Jewish setting, which has always been important to him. His job can be very demanding. In the spring and fall, it is not unusual for him to work a seventy-hour week and still not get everything done.

A typical day for Rabbi Stein might include speaking to a group of three hundred people, counseling a dying man in the hospital, teaching Hebrew to a class of four-year-old children, talking to an excited couple about their approaching marriage, or counseling and referring members of the congregation to specialists for help. As a "teacher," the Rabbi's function is to educate his congregation. He does this in his service as he explains Jewish values, history, ideas, and perspective to his congregation.

Rabbi Stein believes that all clergy, regardless of their denomination, have many things in common. All have one-on-one relationships with people as a major part of their ministry, and all share important moments and rites of passage with their congregations.

A Police Chaplain

Russell T. Schelling just fell into being a police chaplain. He often rode along with a neighbor on his police beat on the midnight shift. These experiences led the police chief to ask him to become a chaplain. In order to handle this job, Russell has had counselor training, Bible college, and training from his pastor. He tries to spend as much time as he can riding with the police officers and just talking to them. He now also participates in their physical agility tests in order to get to know the officers better. Russell has spent fifteen years building relationships with members of the police force, and they call him when they need him.

As a chaplain, Russell enjoys helping the police handle their jobs. One of the things that he likes least about the job is death notifications, which are difficult because people just react, and there is no one right thing to say. He just has to be honest and caring and tell people what has happened.

A Look at the Future

The population growth in the United States has brought about excellent opportunities for people who want careers in professions that traditionally involve a lot of talking. There is an especially great need for teachers in many parts of the country, as well as for clergymen and clergywomen. While articulate people have a great opportunity to talk in these careers, they must invest considerable time in preparing for these careers in order to be able to speak knowledgeably.

CHAPTER SEVEN

Listening and Talking

Advice Givers

Using your talkative nature to help others overcome life's difficulties is very rewarding. Professional advice givers, such as psychologists, psychiatrists, counselors, and social workers, have been trained to help people adjust to life and deal with problems. These are the people who step in to help you, whether you are severely depressed, overwhelmed with stress, hooked on drugs, suffering from grief, uncertain about career or personal decisions, or just need someone to talk to about your problems— large or small. These professionals listen to what you have to say, ask the right questions to give you insight into your difficulties, and provide suggestions that give you the tools to handle your problems. They are talkative people who have learned how to say the right thing to help people resolve their troubles.

Psychologists

Psychologists specialize in many different areas. Some are researchers studying human behavior; however, talkative types are the clinical psychologists. You usually find them working in independent or group practice or in hospitals, clinics, or schools. They help mentally or emotionally disturbed clients adjust to life, help people deal with life stresses, such as divorce or death, and increasingly help medical and surgical patients deal with their illnesses or injuries. On the job, you will find them interviewing patients; giving diagnostic tests; providing individual, family, and group psychotherapy; and designing and implementing behavior modification programs. In their work, they frequently collaborate with doctors and other specialists, which means even more talking on the job.

Educational Requirements and Outlook

Opportunities to work as psychologists are best for those with doctoral degrees in psychology, which is the degree required for employment as a clinical or counseling psychologist. It takes five to seven years of graduate study to earn this degree, and competition is keen for admission into graduate programs. Graduates with master's degrees in psychology encounter competition for the limited number of jobs for which they qualify. Graduates of master's degree programs in school psychology should have the best job prospects, as schools are expected to increase student counseling and mental health services. Bachelor's degree holders can expect very few opportunities directly related to psychology. Those who meet state certification requirements may become high school psychology teachers.

Employment of psychologists is expected to grow because of the need to combat alcohol and drug abuse, marital strife, family violence, crime, and other problems plaguing today's society. Plus, there is an increased emphasis on mental health maintenance in conjunction with the treatment of physical illness and public concern for the development of human resources, including children in school and the growing elderly population.

Earnings

Psychologists with doctoral degrees may expect an average starting salary of about $40,000 in most fields. The starting salaries for holders of master's and bachelor's degrees are usually much lower.

Psychologist Behind Bars

Michael J. Gatton is a clinical psychologist who does not work in a typical setting. His work environment is a windowless office in the bowels of a prison close to the other health care workers in the medical department. His job is an appropriate one for talkative types, as Michael spends 75 percent of the day talking. He has to answer questions and convey in words that he has heard what his patients are saying and then provide them with suggestions and advice that they can understand. He also gives presentations and informational speeches to large groups in the prison. A lot of Michael's work with individuals focuses on determining what the real problem is. Often the real problem, where the change can be made, is not always the apparent problem. For Michael, one of the most difficult aspects of his job is telling patients things they don't want to hear—they don't always want good advice. One of his happiest moments on the job is being able to see someone who was shaky and hanging by a thread really feel better.

Michael finds mental health work, in general, to be very fast paced because he is often hit with emergencies. He says that people expect answers, even when he has limited information and has had insufficient time to think over a situation. In his job, he must be able to assess situations quickly and then move on. Furthermore, patients present problems that have no easy solutions, and he sees people who know less about their mental health than the average person on the street.

There is no such thing as a typical day working in the prison environment. However, Michael usually sees three or four new offenders to discuss their personal problems, and then he sees two or more people whom he is helping work on problems. This is followed by a therapy or education group. Of course, daily emergencies come up, too. His job is always very interesting, and he usually finds it's a real treat to see people who have not had the opportunity to work on their mental health. He likes interacting with people and being able to answer their questions. He also likes teaching. What he likes least about his job is the understaffing of the facility and not always having an answer when he is expected to say something. And he definitely dislikes not having enough time for solitude and reflection. Nevertheless, Michael feels that he is very well suited for the job because he has a natural inclination to help people. He also feels that his present job gives him a sense of meaning and purpose. There is not a lot of competition for his job because not many people truly feel comfortable working in a prison atmosphere.

As early as grade school, Michael knew that he wanted a job that would require a lot of talking. He was always a leader and constantly being called on to be the spokesperson for a group. He feels that he gained his way with words through leadership positions in school and through a lot of years of teaching. Michael cautions those who would like to follow in his footsteps, however, that this is not a job that will make them rich. He also points out that if you don't have a real desire to help people, you won't be able to last in this career.

....

Psychiatrists

Psychiatrists are medical doctors who tend to their patients' mental, emotional, and behavioral symptoms. They treat patients who suffer from mental and emotional illnesses that make it difficult to cope with everyday living or to control their behavior so that it is acceptable in society. Treatment varies according to the individual patient's needs. Psychiatrists may prescribe medication that can alter the patient's feelings or behaviors, such as tranquilizers or antidepressants. Some psychiatrists use medication alone, while others use a combination of medication and behavior therapy. The need for psychiatrists continues to grow as the population grows.

Psychiatry Intern

Jeff Rediger is in the first year of a residency in psychiatry. He has spent six months taking care of the medical and psychiatric needs of people with mental illness. Two months of his year will be spent on a neurology rotation, and four months will be spent in primary care medicine. Right now, he is working on an inpatient psychiatric ward, where he is on call for as long as thirty-six hours at a time about three or four times a month, handling emergency psychiatric problems such as suicide attempts, psychotic episodes, and toxic ingestions in the emergency room. Jeff is required to collect information from people so that he can diagnose and then treat them.

Career Path. Jeff has been a pastoral counselor, a psychiatric assistant, and an at-risk counselor. His educational background includes a bachelor's degree, a master of divinity degree, and a medical degree. After he completes his current internship, he will become a resident at the Harvard Medical School. Although Jeff did not need a degree in divinity, he has found it extremely helpful in preparing for the work he does. What he likes most about having a job that requires a lot of talking—although his job does involve more listening than talking—is sharing ideas with patients and seeing how those ideas can help people.

Acquiring Verbal Skills. Jeff feels that he gained the verbal skills he uses today by reading a lot of the toughest classics, which he believes are the best teachers. He believes that you should study the great ideas that shaped cultures and then work hard to articulate those ideas and form your own critical opinions about the degree of truth they contain. True education, to Jeff, is about the development of character and heart, which helps you become articulate and thoughtful.

Counselors

The first professional counselors were vocational counselors who helped people select careers. Next on the counseling scene were mental health counselors who helped veterans returning from World War II, followed by guidance counselors who initially had the task of helping students plan for college. Today, you can find a job as a counselor serving even more groups of people.

Rehabilitation counselors help people deal with the personal, social, and vocational effects of their disabilities. They counsel people with disabilities resulting from birth defects, illness or disease, accidents, or the stress of daily life.

Employment counselors help people make solid career decisions. This can involve helping them develop job-seeking skills and providing assistance with finding a job.

Mental health counselors work with both individuals and groups in dealing with addiction and substance abuse; family, parenting, and marital problems; stress management; aging; suicide; and other issues of mental and emotional health. Many of these counselors are referred to as therapists.

School counselors work at all levels, from elementary school through college. They may work with individuals, small groups, or entire classes. These counselors also consult and work with parents, teachers, school administrators, school psychologists, school nurses, and social workers. At the elementary level, they do more social and personal counseling and less vocational and academic counseling than those at the secondary level. School counselors help students understand their abilities, interests, talents, and personality characteristics so that they can develop realistic academic and career options. Counselors use interviews, counseling sessions, tests, and other tools when evaluating and advising students. They may operate career information centers and career education programs. Counselors also help students understand and deal with their social, behavioral, and personal problems and provide special services, including alcohol and drug prevention programs and classes that teach students to handle conflicts without resorting to violence.

Training to Be a Counselor

If you decide to become a counselor, you usually need a master's degree in counseling or a related field. In accredited programs, part of your graduate work will involve a period of supervised clinical training. All states require school counselors to hold state school certification, and most are now requiring other counselors to have some form of license, certification, or registry for practicing outside schools. Many counselors are voluntarily certified by the National Board for Certified Counselors, which requires a master's degree, at least two years of supervised counseling experience, and passing the board's national exam.

Earnings

School counselors in elementary and secondary schools earn an average of $51,000 per year. Substance abuse and behavioral disorder counselors earn an average of $32,000 per year. Self-employed counselors and those employed by counselor groups typically earned more than the average.

School Counselor

Fred Chandler enjoys the individual students, parents, and teachers he works with every day as a high school counselor. Like most high school counselors, he works with a great number of students—counseling 340 students, freshmen through seniors. He sees each student at least once a year for fifteen to twenty minutes to discuss educational and career goals, which involves planning the student's schedule of courses or discussing college plans. There are few moments during the day when Fred is not talking to students in his office, contacting parents, or resolving student problems with teachers.

Besides having scheduled conferences with students each day, emergencies may pop up requiring an immediate counseling session with a student on discipline or personal problems. In addition, some time is spent in follow-up counseling sessions with students. And at the beginning of the school year, Fred has longer counseling sessions (forty-five to fifty minutes) with students who have taken career inventory tests and need to go over the results with him. You will find him in front of large groups providing college and career information. He also speaks with groups of parents about school issues. Even though Fred talks a lot on the job, listening to what others say is a very important component of his work as a counselor.

On the job, Fred is careful about what he says because this is one job where talking is not as important as saying the right words. Through counseling sessions, he wants to help students consider alternatives in making decisions. One of his roles is pointing out options; another is simply providing information. At times, Fred may have to point out to students that some of their choices are not realistic. For example, few students with poor grades are ever admitted to Ivy League schools.

Background. Fred taught school for five years, then he obtained his master's degree and became a counselor. He also earned an education specialist degree in counseling. Besides being licensed as a school counselor by the state, Fred is a National Certified Counselor, which requires him to complete one hundred additional hours of professional training every five years. In addition, he has served as the executive director of the Indiana Counseling Association.

Career Advice. Fred points out that it is very important for counselors to be involved throughout their careers in professional development activities in order to keep abreast of what is happening in the field and to constantly upgrade their skills.

Counselor in Private Practice

It is not easy to get a marriage, family, and child counselor (MFCC) license in the state of California. Mary Gail Nelson had to have a master's in counseling or related area plus three thousand hours of internship to become an MFCC. According to Mary Gail, it takes about five to six years to earn a master's degree and obtain a license. She also holds a lifetime teaching credential, which is helpful in working with schoolchildren.

The focus of Mary Gail's practice is marital and relationship counseling. For her, talking on the job means trying to ask good questions that give people insights into themselves or their relationships. It also means helping people clarify issues, and in some cases it means giving advice.

How much Mary Gail speaks during a fifty-minute counseling session varies. She tries to give clients helpful feedback. If parents want help with their children, she may offer considerable advice. In marital counseling, she may play an active role as she helps a couple negotiate solutions and gain insight into their difficulties. At other times, she may talk very little as a client wishes her to reflect upon what he or she is saying or simply understand the particular dilemma or experience.

Career Advice. To become a counselor like Mary Gail, you must not only like to talk to people, you must also like and accept people in their pain. It is very important to be empathetic, as that is one of the qualities that helps in healing people.

Family Therapist

Sherry Rediger has always been interested in understanding other people. In the second grade she often went around interviewing friends and relatives. Finally, in the ninth grade, she found a book about psychology and said, "Oh, wow, there's a name for this!"

Today, as a family therapist, Sherry meets with individuals, couples, and sometimes whole families who are experiencing some kind of life difficulty—usually involving a relationship. She listens a long time and takes a detailed history about each person's relationships, all the way back to stories about grandparents. Sherry helps people understand the problems in their lives as being related to themes, patterns, and stories in their family culture. She helps them decide what has been helpful in their history and what may need healing. Then, together, they work on celebrating the gifts and healing the hurts, which often involves becoming stronger in some ways and softer in others. It's also a lot about forgiveness. In much of her work, the emphasis is on listening rather than talking.

Sherry also works as a supervisor of individuals who are learning to become therapists. She talks with these people about their family histories because it is important for therapists to understand their own problems and strengths. She also discusses with them the work of other therapists.

Career Path. After Sherry earned her bachelor's degree in psychology, she worked as a psychiatric assistant at Philhaven Hospital. She worked mostly with adolescents who had been hospitalized for emotional or psychiatric problems. Many had experienced physical or sexual abuse. Most of her day was spent talking to and doing activities with these teens. Next, she earned a master's degree in family therapy from Hahnemann University. During her time there she worked as a therapist in both inpatient and outpatient settings. Sherry finished her education with a doctorate in marriage and family therapy from Purdue University. Spending years earning degrees is essential for becoming a therapist.

During her career, Sherry has worked primarily in private practice and as a supervisor in several educational settings. She has also taught in a university and written for marriage and family therapy books. At present, she has reduced her work schedule to concentrate on raising her children.

Career Advice. Sherry's advice for anyone wanting to follow her career path is to be prepared to work hard on your own problems and issues. You need to find a balance between being a caregiver and a caretaker. She also points out that you must be tenacious because there is so much academic work. Finally, Sherry advises therapists to find a lot of ways to play and stay lighthearted.

Psychotherapist

Alan J. Schneider is a psychotherapist who helps people help themselves as he guides and teaches them. He provides them with strategies and techniques for overcoming problems and obstacles.

Alan's educational background includes master's and doctoral degrees in education, a master's degree in social work, and five years of psychoanalytic training in hypnotherapy.

On the job, Alan likes talking with people because it provides a tremendous opportunity to learn. However, the downside is it can be repetitive. In the future, Alan sees himself doing more psychotherapy, conducting seminars, and writing and teaching in his field. His advice to young people who want a career like his is to focus more on listening than talking.

Career Path. Alan's first job after high school was as a salesman for a travel agency. His specialty was selling honeymoon packages to newlyweds. When he finished undergraduate school, he taught in the New York school system for one year. From there he went on to become a counselor in a drug rehabilitation center, which led him to become a therapist in the state prison for women in New York. By then he knew that he was a good talker.

....

Social Workers

Unfortunately, there is an incredible number of people who need help. Social workers help people cope with a wide range of problems, including mental illness, inadequate housing, unemployment, lack of job skills, financial mismanagement, serious illness, disability, substance abuse, unwanted pregnancy, and antisocial behavior. They also work with families who have serious conflicts, including those involving child or spousal abuse. Being able to talk to people is more than a benefit for this job—it is an essential prerequisite. Through direct counseling, social workers help clients identify their concerns, consider solutions, and find resources. Social workers also must be able to give people concrete information on such things as where to go for debt counseling, how to find child care or elder care, how to apply for public assistance or other benefits, or how to get an alcoholic or drug addict admitted to a rehabilitation program. In addition, they visit their clients on a regular basis and provide help during crises, so communications skills are extremely important. The nontalking side of this job involves considerable paperwork, from reviewing eligibility requirements to filling out forms and applications.

On the Job

You probably have a bachelor's degree and may even have a master's degree if you are a social worker. You are also most likely to have a government agency as your employer. Although you are only supposed to work a forty-hour week, your hours aren't necessarily confined to nine to five because emergencies frequently occur that may require you to meet with clients on weekends and evenings. You may need to attend community meetings as well. Your workplace could be an office or residential facility; however, many social workers travel locally to visit with clients or meet with service providers. While this work is satisfying, it can be emotionally draining. Furthermore, understaffing and large caseloads add to the pressure in some agencies. Job opportunities are good in this area as the need for social services continues to expand. The average salary for social workers with master's degrees in social work is more than $34,800 per year.

Child Protective Services Social Worker

What Nick Costa has to say as a family reunification/permanency planning caseworker is extremely important because it can have such an impact on children and their families. Most of the children with whom he works are in temporary or long-term foster care. Nick must stay in close communication with them through visits and phone calls to ensure they are being taken care of and to find out if they have any problems. At the same time, he is meeting and talking on the phone with their parents to provide them with information on how they can get needed counseling, enroll in parenting classes, or schedule drug testing. Nick also coordinates parent-child visits and monitors the progress parents are making in following the court-ordered service plan that can lead to family reunification.

Besides talking to the children in foster care and their parents, Nick regularly talks to the foster parents. He often coordinates appointments with them for the children's doctors and therapists as well as for parental visits. And he may discuss with foster parents ways to resolve problems the parents are having with the children. Much time is also spent on the phone talking to doctors, teachers, therapists, and others who are in close contact with the children. In case conferences with superiors, Nick must present the dynamics of a case in an orderly fashion so he can get advice as well as authorization to proceed in a certain direction on the case. Unfortunately, Nick's job is not just a speaking job. He has to document everything that is said to everyone involved in a case as well as everything that he does. This means a lot of paperwork.

Communication Skills. To handle a job like Nick's, you need to be a very skilled communicator who is equally at home talking to a three-year-old child, a psychiatrist, and a parent who didn't complete high school. It is as important to understand the latest slang when talking with children as it is to understand and use technical vocabulary in communicating with professionals. Knowing how to talk to all these people makes it possible to build a rapport with them that can lead to the effective handling of a case.

One other area of communication is very important for family reunification/permanency planning caseworkers—knowing how to speak in a courtroom. When Nick goes to court, which is frequently for review hearings on his cases, he must first prepare a written document summarizing the case and his recommendations for future disposition. Some hearings are informal and the judge simply asks him to make a statement about how the case should be handled. At other times, hearings are more formal, and he is sworn in as a witness. Lawyers argue with caseworkers at times, so Nick has to know how to hold his own verbally when dealing with attorneys.

In his job, Nick deals with very delicate and complicated issues concerning the removal of children from their family homes and the possible future reunification of families. These are emotionally charged issues. By using his verbal skills as well as his professional experience, Nick has been able to forge strong relationships with foster children and excellent rapport with their many caregivers. He has even been able to win the respect of parents whose children have been removed from their home. Nick's background includes a bachelor's degree in social work plus thirteen years of experience as a social worker.

Helping Others Through Words

If you are a talkative person who can listen to others, then a career as a psychologist, psychiatrist, counselor, or social worker may be right for you. Besides your gift of gab, however, you need to be an empathetic person concerned with others' problems. Also, you need to be willing to earn at least a master's degree for almost every one of these jobs. Job opportunities in these careers are good as more attention is being focused on helping people handle emotional and mental problems. It is important to understand that many experience burnout in some of these professions because of the stress of dealing with people in need.

CHAPTER EIGHT

Influencing and Informing

Government Spokespeople

J ust as businesses and organizations have jobs that let people spend their workdays talking, so does the government. In fact, many of these jobs are the same. You can expect jobs such as dispatcher, teacher, lawyer, historic site guide, and psychiatrist in both the public and private sectors to have similar responsibilities. Likewise, there is not much difference between working as a switchboard operator at the White House and at Microsoft or between being a receptionist at the Pentagon and holding the same job title at General Motors.

A few jobs, however, are more closely associated with the government than the private sector. One of these jobs is as a recruiter for the armed forces. Another is as a press secretary, and a third involves working behind the counter in government facilities as one of the thousands of employees who give us licenses, permits, postal supplies, and information. In this chapter, we take a closer look at these three examples of government jobs for talkative types.

Armed Forces Recruiters

Attracting the most qualified employees available and matching them to the jobs for which they are best suited is important for the success of any organization, including the armed forces (U.S.

Army, Navy, Air Force, Marines, and Coast Guard). The job of recruiter has become especially important since the elimination of the draft, which used to provide a steady pool of candidates for all branches of the services. Now the armed forces are competing with the business world to obtain the best possible candidates, and these recruiters play a major role in keeping America strong.

Becoming a Recruiter

First of all, recruiters are members of one of the branches of the armed forces. They may volunteer or be selected on the basis of their records for this position. Most recruiters are enlisted personnel. Once selected for an assignment, they attend recruiting school before being assigned to a recruiting station. The school typically lasts for about two months and is in many ways a course on how to become a successful salesperson. Much attention is focused on helping the recruiter develop excellent communication skills. Emphasis is also placed on how to find recruits. The school teaches future recruiters about the enlistment options, educational opportunities, and occupational specialties available to recruits. The recruiters also learn how to administer a pretest of the qualifying exam in order to give recruits an idea of how they would do on the actual exam. After completing school, the recruiters are assigned to a station where they receive guidance from the station commander. They could be assigned to a small two-recruiter station or one with eight or more recruiters. On the job, they are given a quota that requires them to bring in two or more new recruits each month.

Marine Recruiter

When you first meet Marine Staff Sergeant Dean Rackley, you are immediately struck by his military bearing, crisp uniform, and friendly manner. Dean is a marine recruiter who has the responsibility of finding two new recruits each month for the corps. This is not an easy task in a suburban Northern California county. It means working nine- to ten-hour days, only three of which are spent in his office making phone calls and hosting interviews. The rest of the time Dean is at schools and colleges and wherever he believes he can find people who may be interested in a career in the marines. This can even include walking up to teens on streets and in malls and asking them if they have ever considered joining the marines. Those who express an interest are given his card and invited to come to the recruiting office to learn more about being a marine.

This is decidedly a good job for anyone who likes to meet and talk to new people every day. Although Dean considers himself an introvert, he has become a first-class communicator by mastering the communication skills he was taught at the marine recruiting school, which lasted seven weeks. Besides teaching how to sell the corps, screen candidates, and fill out the paperwork, the training emphasized reading body language, capturing an individual's interest in the first few seconds of contact, and talking with people from very different backgrounds. At the school, Dean also learned how to improve his communication skills by studying the many videos that were taken of his speeches. On the job, he now feels comfortable whether he is speaking formally to large audiences or to individuals he has never met before.

For career marines like Dean, it is almost a necessity to work a stint as a recruiter, drill instructor, or marine security guard in order to advance. After spending two or three years as a recruiter, depending on whether you are a reservist or on active duty, you can extend your tour in this duty.

You can also elect recruiting as your career. Dean is now considering this option as he is quite enthusiastic about his work. He likes dealing with young people who can meet the high requirements of the marines, talking with former marines who are now leaders in his community, and meeting so many people. The special-duty pay, out-of-pocket expense money, and camaraderie of his fellow recruiters are extras he enjoys in this career. But above all else, Dean enjoys being an ambassador for a corps that has served America so proudly.

Press Secretaries and Other Information Providers

The American people are intensely interested in what is going on in the government. They want to know their elected officials' views on issues and about the activities of government agencies and officials. The job titles of people in the government who keep us informed include press secretary, public affairs specialist, information officer, and communications specialist. All of these people interact with media representatives to bring us news about the government. For example, the president's press secretary meets with the media on a daily basis to let us know what issues the president is considering, the names of people he is appointing to federal positions, the bills that he will sign and veto, and even the plans that are being made for a vacation. In the same way, the public affairs specialists in the Department of Energy keep us informed about such matters as the proposed lease of offshore land for oil exploration, miles-per-gallon standards for automobiles, and the safety of nuclear power plants. Press secretaries for members of Congress keep us aware of their elected representatives' accomplishments.

Talking to the media is just one part of the job of keeping the public informed. Press secretaries and other information providers must obtain the information that they relate to us. To do this, they frequently confer with their bosses and other employees and read appropriate materials, from legislation to department papers.

At times, these media experts are called upon to give advice on public relations issues to others in their workplaces. Their jobs usually involve writing press releases, too. In addition, they have to establish and maintain cooperative relationships with representatives of the media, public-interest groups, and political groups. The average salary in the federal government for nonsupervisory, supervisory, and managerial positions in this field is close to $50,000 a year.

The Background Required for Press Secretaries

Although there are no defined standards for entry into a position as an information provider for the government, most individuals in these jobs have college degrees. Their majors do not seem to be important; however, many have majored in journalism, communications, or political science. A high percentage of these government publicists also worked in the media as newspaper, radio, or television reporters covering a government beat. Most have demonstrated solid communications skills, too. This is not typically a first job for someone just out of college, although it is possible to gain experience through internships.

Press Secretary for a Legislator

California is the most populous state in the United States and a land of contrasts—from the glittering world of entertainment in Los Angeles to tremendous farms in rich agricultural regions, some of the largest cities in the nation, barren deserts, high mountains, and forests of ancient redwoods. Its economy is larger than most countries in the world. Within California, as in other states, the legislature is a very important layer of government because it passes laws that have impact on the daily lives of its citizens. One of the most important political figures in California government is Attorney General Bill Lockyer. He also served as the leader of the state senate, with the responsibilities of offering guidance to other senators, ensuring that important legislation passed, and assigning committee members and chairpersons. Senator Lockyer had a full-time press secretary. Other state legislators usually have an individual on staff who handles some of the same responsibilities. Senator Lockyer's press secretary, Sandy Harrison, served as the pipeline between the senator and the reporters covering state government.

On the Job. Much of Sandy's day as a press secretary was spent talking. He talked to Senator Lockyer, to reporters, and to policy people as he strove to convey the senator's message to the public in the best possible way. Phone calls played an important role in his day; reporters constantly called him for news. Rarely was it necessary for him to call them in order to get the senator into the news. Sandy's job, however, was not all talking. He read as many newspapers as possible each day to keep up with what was happening in the state and had to write press releases on bills the senator wanted passed. When the senator traveled, Sandy did not usually accompany him because Lockyer preferred to travel without an entourage. Before a trip, Sandy usually discussed the trip with the senator and gave him material to use in his speeches.

The California legislature is typically in session for eight months a year. Sandy's job was equally important when it was not in session because reporters were still looking for stories. They wanted Lockyer's reaction to the past session as well as his plans for the future. Every other year in California is an election year, when it became Sandy's role to answer reporters' many questions about why the senator and other members of his political party should be reelected. Although he pointed out the differences between Lockyer and his opponent and discussed where the senator stood on issues, Sandy did not work for the campaign.

Being a press secretary means long hours but not unbearably long hours, according to Sandy. He typically worked from 9:00 A.M. to 6:00 P.M. five days a week. A few times a year—at the end of a legislative session, during the budget debate, or on election nights—he worked twenty-eight hours straight.

Becoming a Press Secretary. Sandy had never been a press secretary before he took this position with Senator Lockyer. However, he did know the job from the reporter's side as he had worked in Sacramento for a major California newspaper covering the state capital. His approach to this job was to give the reporters the information that he wanted to know when he was a reporter. This, he believes, was the key to his success as a press secretary.

Sandy did not just bring credentials as a reporter to this job. His qualifications were impressive. After graduating from college with a major in political science, he worked at several radio stations and was on the air doing news reports. Then he switched to print journalism and put out a newspaper in a small community in California before becoming a reporter.

Behind the Counter in Government Offices

Behind the counter in government offices, employees are ready to handle our needs for such diverse things as:

- birth records
- building permits
- death certificates
- dog licenses
- drivers' licenses
- employment information
- food stamp applications
- marriage licenses
- passport applications
- payment of traffic fines
- postal supplies
- social security information
- tax information
- voter registration
- welfare information
- zoning changes

The people who take care of these needs can be employees of city, county, state, or federal units of the government. One thing they all have in common is that a large part of their working day is spent talking to the public, so they must be able to talk with people from all walks of life. At the same time, they must be information experts who can answer the wide variety of questions that come to them each day from the people who stand at their counters. Although their behind-the-counter duties vary widely, most of these government workers greet people and, after determining their needs, either assist them or refer them to someone else who can be of help. They may spend just a few minutes with an individual who wants to register to vote or obtain a passport or birth certificate, or they may spend considerable time with someone trying to resolve a tricky tax question or seeking a building permit. Their responsibilities vary, too, by level of experience.

Postal Clerks

The greatest number of government employees who have jobs behind the counter are postal clerks. These clerks sell stamps, money orders, postal stationery, and mailing envelopes and boxes; weigh packages to determine postage; and check that packages are in satisfactory condition for mailing. They also register, certify, and insure mail and answer questions about postage rates, post office boxes, mailing restrictions, and other postal matters. They also may help customers file claims for damaged packages. From the start to the end of the workday, they have constant contact with the public.

Qualifications. Postal workers have to be at least eighteen years old (or sixteen, if they have a high school diploma). Qualification for a position is based on a written examination. Applicants' names are listed in order of their examination scores. Five points are added to the score of an honorably discharged veteran and ten points to the score of a veteran wounded in combat or disabled. When a vacancy occurs, the appointing officer chooses one of the top three applicants; the rest of the names remain on the list to be considered for future openings until their eligibility expires, usually two years from the examination date.

The Employment Picture. There is such keen competition for positions as postal clerks that few people under twenty-five are hired for this job. Furthermore, most applicants remain on the waiting list for one or two years after passing the examination. Even after getting a job as a postal clerk, it is customary for workers to begin on a part-time or flexible basis before getting full-time employment.

Salaries. Beginning pay for full-time clerks is more than $40,000 a year, which can increase to more than $50,000 with additional experience. Besides the hourly wage and benefits package, some workers receive a uniform allowance.

U.S. Postal Clerk

If you walk into certain post offices, you will notice an innovation—the postal store. It is a separate area in a post office where you can purchase stamps, boxes, envelopes, and other postal products that now include some items of clothing with images of stamps on them. You can also pick up boxes and envelopes for express and priority mail.

George Bailey is a postal clerk working behind the counter in one of these new postal stores. In this job, he really acts as a salesperson. When George first started working in the store, it had only been open a month, so many postal patrons did not realize that they could buy stamps from him instead of waiting in the regular customer line. So George would walk from behind his counter over to the line and tell the people who just wanted stamps or other supplies that he could sell what they needed at the postal store. Now all the regulars at this post office know him, so he has a steady stream of customers. Educating people about all the services that the post office offers is a big part of George's job, which means a lot of talking in the workplace.

Career Path. After retiring from the U.S. Air Force, George took the requisite tests and was hired at the post office as a clerk in mail processing. One day, during a holiday rush period, he was called up front to help people who had come to collect packages. George was delighted to be working and chatting with people and asked the postmaster if he needed any more window clerks. Fortunately, more were needed, so George enrolled in a course for two weeks, passed it with flying colors, worked a week side-by-side with an instructor, and then was on his own behind the counter. When a study showed there were too many window clerks at this post office, George was reassigned to a smaller facility where he is now working in the postal store.

On the Job. When George was a window clerk, knowing how to talk to people was very important. He had to explain postal policies and services, handle angry customers, and exchange brief pleasantries with each customer as he assisted them. In his present job, he not only sells items in the postal store to customers, but he also talks about all the stock available in the store as well as the services that he can provide, such as weighing packages. At times, George also fills in as a window clerk.

George clocks in about fifteen minutes before his shift begins at 8:30 A.M. and picks up money and a stock of stamps. At the end of the day, he has to balance the books for the store just as window clerks have to reconcile their stock and money drawer. His day is supposed to end at 5:15 P.M., but it sometimes takes longer to reconcile money and receipts. Although George is entitled to an hour for lunch, on busy days, especially Mondays, he rarely gets more than thirty minutes.

Becoming a Talkative Type. In high school, George was a quiet student—afraid to speak up and ask questions. But this changed after George joined the air force, completed college, became a supervisor of forty to fifty people, and attended a number of air force schools on managing, where he had to make speeches and give interviews. The schools taught George how to become a communicator and to ask questions when he didn't know the answers.

George also discovered that he truly enjoyed talking to people. One of the reasons he likes his present job is the opportunity to talk with so many different people.

A Glimpse at the Employment Picture

Although the current philosophy is to shrink the budget and reduce the number of government employees, there are decidedly areas with good opportunities for talkative types to find jobs. One is as a recruiter for the armed forces because it has become far more difficult to find young people who are interested in careers in the military. Press secretaries and information providers for government agencies and departments form a small occupation; nevertheless, there remains a need for these people to keep the public informed about the activities of elected officials and various departments of the government. While the post office is becoming more automated, it still has a considerable need for postal clerks because the volume of mail is increasing.

CHAPTER NINE

Talkers Having Fun

Travel, Tourism, and Hospitality Talkers

D id you talk nonstop to family and friends about your last vacation? Do you really enjoy talking about your favorite restaurants, hotels, and clubs? If so, a career in travel, tourism, and hospitality may be just right for you! You will be helping people have a good time. What you say to them and how you say it can enhance their enjoyment, whether you're recommending a meal at a restaurant, a sightseeing tour of the Grand Canyon, or a stay aboard a cruise ship. While you need to be friendly and able to converse with just about everybody, your success in one of these careers also depends on knowing your job well and handling it efficiently. The waiter needs to make patrons feel at a home in a restaurant and at the same time deliver the correct orders to a table. The tour guide has to be able to describe sites in an interesting fashion and still adhere to the day's schedule. The travel agent needs to be able to elicit the traveler's needs as well as make the right reservations.

The future is bright for talkative types who are interested in a career in travel, tourism, and hospitality because it is the fastest-growing industry in the world and the greatest generator of jobs. The field includes entry-level jobs that do not require experience, and it is possible to climb the career ladder rapidly in some jobs. Of course, specialized training beyond high school can usually help you get ahead faster.

Another plus to this career is that you can find a job almost anywhere in the world, from a restaurant in your hometown to a cruise ship or a high-class hotel in New York City or Miami. In addition, along the way you may have the opportunity to talk to politicians, foreign dignitaries (presidents and ambassadors), or movie and TV stars, as well as ordinary citizens.

A Closer Look at Travel Jobs

Travel is glamorous and exciting for both travelers and the people involved in making their trips a success. Sooner or later most travelers come into contact with travel agents, flight attendants, reservationists, and transportation ticket agents. And those who opt for cruises interact with the staff on the ship. These are the people with travel jobs who are the talkers, and many of them are literally nonstop talkers on the job—a perfect situation for talkative types.

Travel Agents

Most travelers at one time or another use a travel agent to arrange a business or personal trip. If it's a business trip, there may not be much conversation between the travel agent and the client other than establishing that the client wants a flight on Friday from Indianapolis that will arrive in Chicago by 9:00 A.M. and wants to return home around 8:00 P.M. the following Wednesday. On the other hand, a personal trip typically requires a great deal of communication. For example, a traveler might want to book a Caribbean cruise for the Thanksgiving holiday. The agent would begin a lengthy conversation to determine that the traveler wants to take his family with two teenagers on a cruise that stops in Cancun, he prefers two staterooms on the third deck, he wants to book several trips ashore, he needs to know what clothing to take and how to tip, and he wants more information on passports. One phone call or visit to the travel agency would not be sufficient to handle all the details. There would be frequent communication to discuss all the plans, including airline reservations, currency exchange rates, shipboard recreation, and seating for dinner. Then if anything serious went wrong on the trip, the travel agent would probably handle frantic phone calls from the anxious clients.

Preparing to Become a Travel Agent

You simply have to know too much to learn on the job how to be a travel agent. Although a few colleges offer bachelor's and master's degrees, most travel agents study two years and earn an associate's degree. Vocational schools also have courses, and it is possible to take a correspondence course from the American Society of Travel Agents. One of the key skills future travel agents must acquire is the ability to operate airline reservations systems.

On the Job with a Travel Agent

Women far outnumber men as travel agents. One of these women is Sylvia Porter, who has been a travel agent for more than ten years. After graduating from college with a bachelor's degree in English, Sylvia had the unusual job of training teachers from around the world to operate a device that allows the blind to read by feeling print. This job, which involved some travel in the United States as well as a trip to Greece, instilled in Sylvia a desire to pursue a career that involved travel. To prepare for a career as a travel agent, she enrolled in a community college and received an associate's degree in tourism.

Sylvia had no difficulty in securing her first job in a small travel agency with three agents. She was older, and in this profession age is considered a plus. At this agency, Sylvia primarily handled leisure clients, selling tours and creating foreign travel packages for those who wanted to travel independently. She also assisted clients who walked in the door while building a client base of repeat customers.

Sylvia was known as an inside agent because she received an hourly salary and no commission. After one year, this agency folded, and Sylvia was seeking a job again.

In her next job, she became an outside agent, which means that her income was based solely on commissions that she split with the agency. No longer did she have the luxury of being assigned walk-in clients; now she had to attract her own clients. Sylvia spent most of her time working with private clients, helping them make leisure travel plans, although she did have some corporate accounts. After five years, however, this firm also folded. Unfortunately, this is one of the downsides of a career as a travel agent—many firms go out of business each year.

Again, Sylvia was able to find a job easily as a travel agent. In her present job, she is working as an outside agent. Although she works independently, the four other agents in the firm cover for each other so that all of them are able to take vacations and still serve their clients.

Talking on the Job. About 75 percent of Sylvia's time on the job is spent talking—much of it to clients. She has to ferret out exactly what they want: Is it budget or elegant accommodations? Is it an all-inclusive tour? Is it sightseeing or lazing by a pool? When she isn't talking to clients on the phone or in person, she is busy calling reservationists to obtain the tours, tickets, and accommodations her clients want. Sylvia also visits with representatives from airlines and tour companies who come to the agency, and part of her time is spent sharing information with her colleagues.

Sylvia truly likes the talking aspect of being a travel agent because she has always been a chatterer. What she dislikes is having a miscommunication with a client or reservationist.

The Pluses and Minuses of Being a Travel Agent

Among the great appeals of a career as a travel agent are the "fam" trips that let agents familiarize themselves with foreign cities, new resorts, tours, and cruises. Agents usually have to pay a small amount for these trips. Also, they frequently have the opportunity to get free or deeply discounted airline tickets for themselves and a companion.

Travel agents earn an average of $27,600 per year. The best-paying jobs go to those who work at agencies focusing on corporate travel. Although the industry projects that the amount of leisure travel is increasing rapidly, suggesting a continuing need for more travel agents, the downside is that many people now get their tickets and make reservations online and through electronic ticketing machines.

Flight Attendants

From the moment the first passenger comes aboard a plane until the last one leaves, flight attendants are almost always talking. Passengers need to be greeted, helped to their seats, instructed in safety procedures, and asked what type of beverages and meals they want and whether they need blankets, pillows, or headsets. Then there are jittery passengers who need to be calmed and passengers with all kinds of questions to be answered.

What It Takes to Be a Flight Attendant

Airlines want loquacious people like you who can speak to strangers in a poised, tactful, and friendly manner. To get this job, you must be at least nineteen years old, fall into a specific weight range depending upon your height, and have excellent health, good vision, and the ability to speak clearly. You must have a high school diploma, but your prospects for getting this job are better if you have attended college or have several years of experience dealing with the public.

Once an airline hires you as a flight attendant, you must attend the airline's own school or one operated by another airline. In the four to six weeks of intensive training, you learn emergency procedures; flight regulations and duties; company operations and policies; and how to prepare meals, handle the beverage service, speak on the intercom, and deal effectively with passengers. In order to fly international routes, you receive additional instruction in passport and customs regulations and dealing with terrorism.

After you complete training, you are assigned to a base. You are usually placed in "reserve status," which means you might be called on short notice to staff extra flights or to fill in for those attendants who are sick or on vacation. It typically takes a year to advance from reserve status to a full-time position.

Earnings

Beginning flight attendants generally earn about $15,500. The average pay for all flight attendants is $43,400 per year. Attendants receive additional compensation for working holidays, night flights, and international fights. They also enjoy free or deeply discounted fares for themselves and their families.

In the Air with a Flight Attendant

Linda Curtis Olinger flies international routes for United Airlines. Let's go aboard a flight from San Francisco to Hong Kong in the first-class cabin to see how much talking she does on a typical flight. Once passengers begin to arrive (they don't all arrive at once), she welcomes them to the flight, volunteers to help them stow their gear, offers them a beverage, and demonstrates safety procedures. Then it is time to sit down for takeoff.

Once it is safe to do so, Linda gets up and checks on her passengers to see if they are warm enough because the cabin can become cool. It's also time to serve beverages, take entrée orders, and hand out headsets to those who wish to see movies. How much she talks to individual passengers depends entirely on how receptive they are to conversation. Some passengers bury themselves in work for the entire flight and want minimal conversation. Vacationers, however, usually like to chat. The dinner service takes approximately three hours to complete. While preparing and cleaning up after the meal, the flight attendants usually talk a lot to each other because they are very sociable people. After dinner, the attendants take turns having a break, which means Linda takes a stint as the only attendant in the cabin. During this time, she is busy serving beverages and selling duty-free merchandise. Before the flight is over, she and the other attendants serve a snack in the middle of the night and another meal one and one-half hours before landing.

After the plane has landed in Hong Kong, Linda helps the passengers gather their belongings and says good-bye to them as they leave the plane. Linda often finds that businesspeople who work intently on their way to Hong Kong want to talk a great deal on the trip home. Some even follow her into the galley after the dinner service to chat about business and family. As you can see, Linda spends most of her flight time talking to the passengers as she meets their needs.

Reservationists and Transportation Ticket Agents

Millions of Americans travel by plane, train, bus, and car every year. When they make reservations for travel or accommodations, purchase tickets, check their luggage, or board a plane, they often deal with reservationists and/or transportation ticket agents. For someone with the gift of gab, these are absolutely ideal jobs because you get to talk to several hundred people each day as well as get your foot in the travel industry door. It's an interesting job, too, because you never know what the next person on the phone or in a line of customers will be like.

To be a reservationist or transportation ticket agent, you need formal training in company policies and procedures in order to answer the many questions you will be asked. You also need specific computer skills. Expect to face considerable competition for these positions because they have minimal entry requirements and are considered a good way to get a start in the airline or travel business. You also should anticipate that you may have to start in a part-time position before getting full-time work. Many entry-level jobs require employees to work irregular shifts. Reservationists earn an average of $27,700 per year, with entry-level employees earning $17,700 per year. Experienced reservationists can earn up to $45,100 per year.

An Experienced Reservationist

Carol Love is an experienced reservation agent working in domestic sales for a major airline. Her current shift is from 3:00 P.M. to 11:30 P.M. Sunday through Thursday. On workdays, she must arrive at the reservations center located near a major airport in time to run her card through a reader, get work gear from her locker, and be at a work station by precisely 3:00 P.M. Her gear consists of a new state-of-the-art headset, which prevents customers from hearing any background noise, and a company manual with reference telephone numbers and information on how to access different computer entries. Her workplace is a large room with stations for about 125 agents. When the company has a special sales promotion, all the stations are filled.

Once Carol puts on her headphones and sits down in front of her computer terminal, the company expects her to be plugged into the phone 95 percent of the time when she is not on break. Her average is a high 97 percent. Her customers can be from anywhere in the United States. Carol does not deal exclusively with customers wanting to purchase tickets, although that is certainly the most common call she receives. Carol also provides information to people who cannot or do not want to use the automated flight information system. During periods of bad weather, she answers a lot of questions about plane arrivals and departures and the cancellation of flights. And she refers callers who have complaints or compliments about airline employees or policies to customer relations.

After her shift starts, the phone calls never stop coming. Only occasionally are there lags between calls. During a call, Carol may chat a little with a customer to make the call more personal, if it seems appropriate. She usually averages five minutes on each call, although she once had a call that lasted one and a half hours. The company goal is for agents to spend three minutes per call. Carol spends the extra time because she wants to be sure her customers understand all aspects of purchasing a ticket, including whether the ticket can be changed or is refundable. The calls that take the most time are those where certificates are being used for discounted fares and companion travel. Although Carol's call time is above average, this is not frowned upon by the company because she sells a lot of tickets.

Transportation Ticket Agent

You can find a job as a transportation ticket agent standing behind a counter at an airport, train, or bus station, but most of these jobs are at airports. On the job, you will talk to travelers as you sell them tickets, assign them seats, and check their baggage. You could also answer questions, give directions, examine passports and visas, and even check in animals. If you work at a boarding gate at an airport, your job would be to check tickets, assign seats, make boarding announcements, and give special assistance to passengers requiring it.

Tourism Talkers

When people are on vacation, they visit tourist attractions such as Monticello, Graceland, Yosemite National Park, New York City, Colonial Williamsburg, Niagara Falls, and Carlsbad Caverns. Many want to know as much as they can about an attraction, and this is the job of tour guides. They lead tourists through attractions as they describe them. To be an effective guide, you must be knowledgeable about every aspect of an attraction. This means committing to memory facts, dates, names, and significant events.

You must also be a skilled speaker who can keep an audience's attention. It helps to blend humor and unique or unusual pieces of information into your presentation. On many tours, you also have to be very skillful to keep the attention and interest of an audience that ranges from preschoolers to senior citizens.

Jobs for tour guides truly vary. You could lead tourists through San Simeon, the home of publishing magnate William Randolph Hearst, and talk about all the famous people who visited him in this castle. You might be aboard a boat circling Manhattan, describing the sites and relating the history of New York City. You could lead tourists on a trip through Europe or Australia, or you could guide adventurers through the Grand Canyon on a raft. The possibilities are endless. Your job might be full-time at a tourist attraction that is open all year or part-time for a park open only in the summer. You could repeat the same information on several tours in a day, or you could be describing different places every day on a longer tour. Nevertheless, one thing is always the same— tour guides talk a lot.

Adventure Tour Leader

For most of the year, Ali Celik leads small groups of tourists on adventure tours through Turkey that involve a lot of hiking. As a child, Ali was fascinated by the history of Turkey, and he continues to love reading about the country so he can relate interesting tales of its past to different tour groups. At each of the many archeological sites the group visits, Ali outlines its place in the country's history and describes what is being seen. On bus trips between sites, he talks to the group over the intercom about current politics, the geography of the country, the Muslim religion, and even about how to bargain with local vendors. From early morning breakfast to evening events, Ali is always talking to the entire group or to individuals on the tour.

You must love to talk and truly like people to handle this job. You also need to be able to keep the tour running smoothly, whether it is making sure all the luggage is picked up, making alternative plans for a meal when a restaurant is closed, or finding another bus if the regular tour bus breaks down.

To make sure that every member of a tour has an enjoyable trip, Ali meets with each one at the start of the tour to find out what he or she wants to get out of the experience. Then at the end of the tour, he always asks the group what they liked about it and how it could be improved. For Ali, every tour is enjoyable because each group is different and has different interests. Before beginning his touring career, Ali graduated from college and then took a special course to become a tour guide.

Ranger Naturalist in Yosemite National Park

After working in Yellowstone National Park and on several other assignments, Shelton Johnson became a ranger naturalist at Yosemite, giving him the opportunity to talk to tourists throughout the year about the wonders of nature in the park. His day begins at 11:30 A.M. when he goes to work at the visitor center in the park. At first, his time is spent doing program development work and handling mail and correspondence. Then he is out on the floor of the visitor center answering questions, from the difficulty of various hiking trails to the name of a flower or bird a visitor saw on a walk. He may also help people find a place to stay or orient them to their new surroundings. Next, Shelton prepares for his nature walk and then leads a ninety-minute tour. Then he returns to the visitor center for another work session. His day ends after he leads another ninety-minute walk.

....

Hospitality Talkers

You'll find jobs in hospitality at restaurants, hotels, and motels. Although every job at these establishments contributes to making customers' visits enjoyable, only those individuals working in front-of-the-house jobs really talk to the customers. In sit-down restaurants, these employees are the waiters and waitresses and hosts and hostesses, while at fast-food restaurants, they are the order takers. At hotels and motels, they are the desk clerks and concierges. The success of most hotels, motels, and restaurants depends greatly on the hospitable treatment their customers receive from these employees.

Waitress at a Family Restaurant

At the sit-down restaurant where Sarah Cravens worked right after college, it was absolutely essential for the waitresses to make customers feel at home. When a family sat at one of her tables, she immediately brought a place mat and crayons to the children and initiated a friendly conversation. If the family had packages, she might ask if they had been shopping. If they were all wearing coats and scarves, Sarah would inquire about how they were surviving the cold weather. One real benefit of getting to know the customers was that it made it easier to remember their orders. Although this was her first job as a waitress, Sarah soon discovered that she was handling it well as many people returned to the restaurant and requested her tables. Seeing the same customers again and again made the job enjoyable for her.

Training. Like most beginning waitresses, Sarah received her training on the job. For a couple of weeks, she followed an experienced waitress around, gradually picking up skill after skill as she assisted her. Sarah learned how to greet customers, describe the daily specials, serve food and beverages, give orders in the kitchen, set tables, and serve large parties. Then she served tables in this waitress's section under her supervision before going out on her own.

Sarah's Earnings. Like most waitresses and waiters at sit-down restaurants, Sarah derived her earnings from a combination of hourly wages and customer tips. Although it wasn't the practice at her restaurant, at many restaurants waiters and waitresses contribute a portion of their tips to a tip pool, which is distributed among many of the establishment's other food-service workers and kitchen staff.

Hostess at an Upscale Italian Restaurant

If you have been to this white-tablecloth Italian restaurant several times, hostess Tami Morgan will recognize you. In fact, she will even recognize your voice on the phone when you call. With Tami, it is always more than, "Hi, how are you?" with customers. She tries to initiate a personal conversation with them to encourage their returning to the restaurant because they've had a good experience.

While being a gregarious person is an absolute essential for this job, it is also necessary to have excellent organizational skills. For example, on a typical Friday evening, Tami may have as many as twenty people waiting for seats. She needs to know the wait time for tables and how to react when things change. If the kitchen gets buried, she has to slow the seating. She is always absolutely honest with customers about how long they will have to wait and immediately updates them if this time should increase. For Tami, this job is like being on a stage as she tries to make the customers happy.

On the job, she warmly welcome guests, assigns them to tables suitable for the size of their group, escorts them to their seats, and provides menus. As the restaurant's personal representative to patrons, she tries to ensure that the service is prompt and courteous. Tami also schedules dining reservations, arranges parties, and organizes any special services that are required.

Gaining Experience. Most hosts and hostesses have had prior experience in restaurants as waiters and waitresses, and Tami is no exception. She started at the age of sixteen as a bus girl and just loved the work, becoming a waitress when she was eighteen.

When the first restaurant she worked for closed, Tami became a waitress, bartender, and floor manager at another restaurant. She was in charge of hiring and firing staff, training, and ordering wine. In her next job, she became a hostess. Like most hosts and hostesses, she learned this job by observation and filling in from time to time for the full-time host or hostess. Today, Tami is an experienced hostess and also a part-time manager at the restaurant where she works.

Front Desk Clerk

Josh Anderson has the friendly, outgoing personality and desire to serve people that front desk clerks must have. He is also well groomed and polite and has a good memory for faces and names. Josh is currently in school studying hospitality management while working an eight-hour day, five days a week. His shift varies; one day he may work from 2:00 P.M. until 10:00 P.M., while another day his work schedule is from 7:00 A.M. to 3:00 P.M. Being a desk clerk is a starting position for managerial trainees at many large lodging facilities, including the hotel where Josh works.

On the job, Josh usually works with another clerk at the front desk. His responsibilities include checking guests in and out, fulfilling guest requests, taking reservations, and assisting all management personnel. Josh received his training on the job— primarily from coworkers but also from the manager. According to Josh, the requirements for this job are people skills, problem-solving skills, and basic computer skills. The average income for starting clerks, like Josh, is about $350 per week.

The Job of Concierge

In the past, concierges were usually multilingual hotel staff members in Europe who handled luggage and mail, made reservations, and arranged tours. Today, many American hotels have this staff position. Concierges are the question answerers who try to make hotel guests feel at home, whether they are telling them the dining room hours or how they can get a suit cleaned immediately. Concierges give directions to tourist attractions and offices, make theater and tour suggestions and reservations, and reserve limousines for hotel patrons. They have to be very knowledgeable about the area and what it offers. They also have to be articulate people who can talk to anyone.

Considering a Career in Travel, Tourism, or Hospitality

Whether you are suggesting a delectable entrée on the menu of a restaurant, describing the activities to be experienced on the cruise ship, or explaining the history and significance of a national park, talking is all part of the fun when your job is to help people enjoy themselves. The fields of travel, tourism, and hospitality are full of opportunities for talkative types who can efficiently help others experience the world.

One of the best ways to become acquainted with the vast number of careers in these areas is by taking a part-time job. This lets you see what so many jobs in hotels, motels, restaurants, tourist attractions, and airlines are like. And it also lets you assess whether a career in one of these areas is right for you.

CHAPTER TEN

More Jobs for Talkative Types

Some people have the gift of gab and just love to talk. If you are one of these people, then you owe it to yourself to find a job that lets you chat, converse, discuss, negotiate, or otherwise run on from nine to five. This chapter introduces several more careers that allow you to be a veritable chatterbox at work.

A Few More Suggestions

There are still more careers than have been mentioned so far that are good choices for talkative types. In fact, wherever you find a business or occupation that involves dealing with people, more than likely there are jobs for people like you who have the gift of gab. When you look at the want ads, search for positions that are looking for people with excellent communication skills. One of these jobs may match your abilities and also give you a splendid opportunity to display your impressive verbal skills. Here are a few more satisfying career ideas.

Find a Chatty Job in Your Current Workplace

Sometimes you can just fall into a truly chatty job where you are working. This is what recently happened to Ann Gisler, an accounting technician who was hired to process travel claim vouchers. This work had always been handled through the mail and on the computer; however, the office decided to set up a phone line so that people who were having difficulty receiving their money could call in and get the problem resolved. Ann was selected for this new position. She was so good at the job and helped so many grateful people that talking on the phone is now her full-time job, and she loves it! So keep your eyes open when you have a job, and you may discover that there are positions in your workplace that literally let you talk all day. Ann has discovered one of those jobs in her workplace and knows that when she completes college, she wants another job that lets her chat at work.

Tutor and Tutor Trainer

For the past twenty years, James Franklin has tutored within the confines of traditional education. This meant talking for hours on end as he explained, reinforced, and then reviewed reading, writing, language, and arithmetic with the people he tutored. Those years of tutoring provided James with the necessary skills to become a trainer of tutors in the Gateway program, which is a basic literacy program designed to motivate learners to continue working on improving their literacy. As a tutor trainer, James instructs tutors, but he also has the responsibility of finding additional tutors, which calls for more talking. In the future, he sees himself becoming a Gateway national trainer as well as heading his own tutoring program for adults, which means he will still be spending his days talking on the job. James points out that tutors must display the patience of Job and the understanding of Solomon to be successful.

Talking Toward a Career Change

Just being interested in talking, enjoying talking, and having a true gift of gab slowly steered Judy Johnson into her present jobs. Of course, getting a bachelor's degree in communications and management also influenced her decision to find a job in which she could chatter all day. Talking seems to give her energy, and Judy also likes all the information she picks up from having conversations with others.

Judy has worked in secretarial jobs and been an insurance agent and office manager. Today, one of Judy's jobs is as a literacy coordinator at a library, where she gives presentations to civic groups about tutoring for adult learners. She also makes phone calls to prospective tutors and learners and schedules adult literacy programs for the library. Judy says, "I do programs and press releases, so I speak and write a lot." Judy also works part-time as a sales representative selling a handheld computer game. On this job, she talks to people interested in the product and explains the product to them in detail. Because of her love of chatting, Judy sees herself making a success of a full-time sales career in the future.

Bridge Director and Teacher

Catherine Lindholm directs bridge games—that is, she runs games involving many players. She is also a bridge teacher who explains the concepts of the game of bridge to adult students. What Catherine likes about having a job that requires a lot of talking is the interaction among the players. This is the fun of working with or teaching adults, she believes. Her advice to young people who might want to follow her career path is to go into teaching only if you really love it. She feels that she gained the verbal skills she uses today as a young child in her home because her parents were very articulate.

Law Enforcement Officer

Officer Douglas Milligan thinks that the most important skill in police work is being able to communicate. It all boils down to words and how effectively you use them, according to Douglas. In his present job as a special deputy at a high school, he spends 90 percent of his shift talking. He uses his verbal skills in interviewing people, asking questions to solve problems, being a mediator, and giving directions. As a mediator, Douglas tries to find out the truth as he plays a neutral role between the individuals involved in a situation. He believes that good verbal communication is everything in getting his job done. Douglas feels that all but one (driving a truck) of his previous jobs helped him acquire the solid verbal skills that he uses today. He has been a fast-food restaurant employee, a bagger at a grocery store, a military police officer, and a security guard. To become a police officer, he took a twelve-week course at the Indiana Law Enforcement Academy and has also taken SWAT team, CPR, and first-aid training. In the future, he sees himself possibly becoming a law enforcement instructor or detective—both jobs for talkative types. Douglas says that future law enforcement professionals need to have good morals and ethics, be physically fit, and be skilled communicators.

Lobbyist

Lobbyists must be very persuasive people as they try to convince legislators to vote in a particular way. A lobbyist can be merely a member of a group interested in a particular law or a paid agent of a group that wants to see a bill passed or defeated. Lobbyists also may try to influence officials in local and state governments and the federal government. Many lobbyists are lawyers. Most work in Washington, D.C., and state capitals.

James M. Gutting is a lobbyist who tries to persuade state and local governments to develop new legislation on authorized government contracts. He is also an attorney who represents people before government agencies for licensing and various appeals. James advises young people to take on a variety of activities to gain job experience. This lets you find out what you don't like and gravitate to the things you do like.

Hairstylist

When people get their hair cut, colored, or styled, they naturally want skilled hairstylists, but they also usually want someone with whom they can talk. Shirlee Semerdjian is a hairstylist. She is also a talkative type who knows what her clients in an upscale shop want to talk about. First of all, she keeps track of what is going on in the world as well as on the local social scene because this interests her clients. In addition, Shirlee is always ready to talk about current movies, the hairstyles of movie and television stars, and what is going on in the lives of her clients. Through continuing classes and seminars, Shirlee keeps up with the newest and latest techniques so she can discuss hair and hairstyles with her clients as well as be up-to-date in her profession. Talking with clients is not the only talking that Shirlee does in this job. She contacts personal shoppers in stores and concierges in hotels who might send her new clients and further build her business. This actually led to her styling the hair of Princess Margaret of England.

Shirlee points out that the business of hairstyling is one of personal involvement. You must remember the styles your clients have worn over the years as well as what they have told you about their lives and families. You also have to learn to acquire intimate speech, which means talking in such a way that you cannot be overheard in the adjoining booth. Because Shirlee enjoys talking and is an excellent conversationalist along with being a skilled hairstylist, her days at the salon are always fully booked.

To become a hairstylist, it is essential to hold a state license, which you can apply for after graduating from a state-licensed barber or cosmetology school and passing a written test. Shirlee went to beauty school as part of an extended program while she was in high school and then passed the state test, which included an examination on theory as well as actually working on people. Hairstylists typically receive their incomes either from straight commissions or from a combination of wages and tips.

Merchandise Manager

You don't have to be in sales at a retail store to have a job that involves a lot of talking. Sam Ingram is a merchandise manager at a huge discount stationery store. He talks all day to customers, employees, and district managers as he handles his job of getting the merchandise to the customers and out the door. Because his duties include counseling employees, mediating customer complaints, and acting as a liaison between the district manager and the employees, he is constantly in a talk, talk, talk mode.

Prior experiences have given Sam the verbal skills he uses on the job. When he was just eighteen, Sam competed in track events in stadiums with as many as ten thousand people watching. As a track star, he often had to give press interviews. This taught him how to deal with stress, pressure, and speaking to the public. As an assistant manager in training at another discount store, Sam attended "Interpersonal Management and Employee Care" seminars that were instrumental in honing his skills in counseling employees, communicating with employees on a daily basis, dealing with angry customers, and interacting with management. On-the-job experience at other large discount stores taught him more about being a good communicator in the workplace. In fact, Sam says that he learned a great deal from just realizing how much he didn't know. Sam believes that talkative types who want to be in management positions should take classes in college that force them to debate, discuss, and just plain talk to prepare for the business world.

The Medical Profession

Many jobs within the medical profession, in addition to the medical doctors discussed in Chapter 6, decidedly involve a lot of talking. In fact, almost anyone who works all day with patients probably needs to be a skilled communicator.

Hospital Nurse

Michael Gilmore is a nurse who must do a lot of talking to handle his job. For example, assessing a patient's needs requires him to ask questions in great detail to solicit the maximum amount of information. He also must give careful instructions to patients and coordinate their care by talking to family, other health care professionals, and service providers. As a nurse, Michael especially likes interacting as part of a team. Michael reminds future nurses that they should have a strong desire to help others and be willing to provide quality service.

Respiratory Therapist

Terrie L. Gilmore works as a respiratory therapist in a management position. Several aspects of her job involve talking with others. She updates or passes on information to the respiratory and nursing staffs and teaches CPR classes. Screening and evaluating patients means talking to the patients and their families, obtaining case histories, and discovering patients' current concerns and goals. Terrie also gives instructions to patients and families on how to properly use respiratory medications and equipment. Finally, she interacts with doctors, nurses, and other therapy team members in helping patients.

In high school, Terrie became acquainted with the medical world by assisting a physical therapist in the rehabilitation of patients. Her educational background includes associate's and bachelor's degrees in respiratory therapy. She is a Registered Respiratory Therapist (RRT). This certification is obtained by passing an examination and is usually required for those in supervisory positions.

Administrative Assistant at an HMO

Anna Zarins is the daughter of Russian immigrants. As a child, when anyone came to the door during the day, her homemaker mother would rely on her to translate. Being required to talk as a child turned her into a person with a gift of gab. Today, she is an administrative assistant at an HMO, where she has to communicate effectively with others, including medical directors, physicians, and the marketing department. It is also her responsibility to talk to irate HMO members who call in for a variety of reasons, from dissatisfaction with their care to requesting help in solving a problem. In this career, as in past careers, conversation has always played a big role. Some days, Anna talks so much that her jaws get tired!

Still More Careers

The more you talk to people about the different kinds of careers they have, the longer your list of careers for talkative types will be. For those with the gift of gab, learning more about careers is really just an opportunity to converse. Here are a few more careers to investigate:

- admitting clerk
- auctioneer
- bank teller
- claims adjuster
- coach
- manicurist
- mediator
- nursing aide
- politician
- product demonstrator
- railroad conductor
- trainer
- union organizer

An Overview of Job Opportunities

The future is bright for talkative types seeking jobs. Being skilled in verbal communication is a valued asset in today's job market. More than two million teachers will be hired in the next ten years due to increased student enrollment and the retirement of an aging teaching force. Firms are clamoring for telemarketers to sell products over the phone and salespeople to work in stores. Restaurants are actively recruiting waiters, waitresses, and hosts to handle the increasing desire of people to eat out more frequently.

More psychologists and counselors are needed to help people handle the demands of the modern world. Of course, there are some areas, such as radio, television, and politics, where you will face keen competition to get the chatty job you want. Most talkative types and others with the gift of gab, however, should be able to find careers that allow them to exercise their proclivity and ability to talk.

Professional Associations

One way to learn more about careers for talkative types is by writing or phoning organizations that have career or employment information. You may wish to contact some of the following associations.

Glamour Talkers in the Limelight

Broadcast Education Association
1771 N Street NW
Washington, DC 20036
www.beaweb.org

International Association of Speakers Bureaus
7150 Winton Drive
Indianapolis, IN 46268
www.igab.org

Radio-Television News Directors Association
1600 K Street NW, Suite 700
Washington, DC 20006
www.rtnda.org

····························

Sales Talkers

Independent Insurance Agents of America
127 South Peyton Street
Alexandria, VA 22314
www.iiaa.org

LIMRA International
PO Box 203
Hartford, CT 06141
www.limra.com

Manufacturers' Agents National Association
One Spectrum Pointe, Suite 150
Lake Forest, CA 92630
www.manonline.org

Manufacturers' Representatives Educational Research
  Foundation
8329 Cole Street
Arvada, CO 80005
www.mrerf.org

National Association of Realtors
430 North Michigan Avenue
Chicago, IL 60611
www.realtor.org

National Retail Federation
325 Seventh Street NW, Suite 1100
Washington, DC 20004
www.nrf.com

Talkers in Businesses and Other Organizations

American Society for Training and Development
1640 King Street, Box 1443
Alexandria, VA 22313
www.astd.org

International Association of Business Communicators
One Hallidie Plaza, Suite 600
San Francisco, CA 94102
www.iabc.com

Public Relations Society of America, Inc.
33 Maiden Lane, Eleventh Floor
New York, NY 10038
www.prsa.org

Telephone Talkers

Communications Workers of America
Research Department
501 Third Street NW
Washington, DC 20001
www.cwa-union.org

United States Telephone Association (USTelecom)
607 Fourteenth Street, Suite 400
Washington, DC 20005
www.ustelecom.org

....

Talking Professions

American Bar Association
321 North Clark Street
Chicago, IL 60610
www.abanet.org

American Federation of Teachers AFL-CIO
555 New Jersey Avenue NW
Washington, DC 20001
www.aft.org

Association for Childhood Education International
17904 Georgia Avenue, Suite 215
Olney, MD 20832
www.acei.org

Association of American Law Schools
1201 Connecticut Avenue NW, Suite 800
Washington, DC 20036
www.aals.org

National Council of Churches of Christ in the U.S.A.
475 Riverside Drive, Suite 880
New York, NY 10115
www.ncccusa.org

Individuals seeking information about religious careers should contact their own local religious organizations.

Advice Givers

American Counseling Association
5999 Stevenson Avenue
Alexandria, VA 22304
www.counseling.org

American Medical Association
515 North State Street
Chicago, IL 60610
www.ama-assn.org

American Psychiatric Association
1000 Wilson Boulevard, Suite 1825
Arlington, VA 22209
www.psych.org

American Psychological Association
750 First Street NE
Washington, DC 20002
www.apa.org

National Association of Social Workers
750 First Street NE, Suite 700
Washington, DC 20002
www.socialworkers.org

Government Spokespeople

Each of the military services has career information available at all recruiting stations. For information about U.S. Postal Service careers, contact:

American Postal Workers Union
1300 L Street NW
Washington, DC 20005
www.apwu.org

Travel, Tourism, and Hospitality Talkers

Information about job opportunities with a particular airline and the qualifications required may be obtained by writing to the human resources manager of the company. For additional information, contact:

American Society of Travel Agents
Education Department
1101 King Street, Suite 200
Alexandria, VA 22314
www.astanet.com

Association of Flight Attendants–CWA
501 Third Street NW
Washington, DC 20001
www.afanet.org

National Restaurant Association Educational Foundation
175 West Jackson Boulevard, Suite 1500
Chicago, IL 60604
www.nraef.org

About the Authors

M arjorie Eberts and Margaret Gisler have been writing professionally for thirty-one years. They are prolific freelance authors with more than ninety books in print, including twenty-one books on careers. The two authors have also written textbooks, beginning readers, study skills books for schoolchildren, and a college preparation handbook. In addition, they write "Dear Teacher," a nationally syndicated education advice column for parents.

Writing this book was a special pleasure for the authors as it gave them the opportunity to talk to so many chatty people who were delighted to talk at length about their careers. Since both authors are quite chatty themselves, they truly enjoyed researching the careers described in this book.

Eberts is a graduate of Stanford University, and Gisler is a graduate of Ball State and Butler Universities. Both received their specialist degrees in education from Butler University. Gisler recently completed a doctorate in education at Ball State University.